# GLASGOW STATIONS

## COLIN JOHNSTON & JOHN R HUME

'*Your train is gliding now through the squalid heart of the city; then it slackens speed, and as you yawn and collect your wraps, it rumbles out on a bridge, the darkness lifts, and for a moment of time a vision lies before you, seen through the twinkling lattice of the girders. It is of a short reach in a river, of water coloured a faint greenish bronze, of a dusky West Highland sunset lingering overhead . . . of huddled silhouettes of vessels moored in midstream or coaling at wharves, of brown smoke and sudden lights blinking out along the quays . . . Another moment and your train rumbles over the bridge, and a swarming, nocturnal city leaps up on every hand to welcome you.*'

James Hamilton Muir, *Glasgow in 1901*

DAVID & CHARLES

NEWTON ABBOT  LONDON  NORTH POMFRET (VT)

Stevenson
19-1-80

To the memory of Donald A. Matheson and his staff, whose foresight and imagination gave Glasgow one of the great British stations.

**British Library Cataloguing in Publication Data**

Johnston, Colin
  Glasgow stations.
  1. Railroads—Scotland—Glasgow—Stations
  I. Title    II. Hume, John Robert
  385'.34          TF302.G/

  ISBN 0–7153–7569–5

Photoset and printed in Great Britain
by Redwood Burn Limited, Trowbridge & Esher
for David & Charles (Publishers) Limited
Brunel House    Newton Abbot    Devon

Published in the United States of America
by David & Charles Inc
North Pomfret    Vermont 05053    USA

# CONTENTS

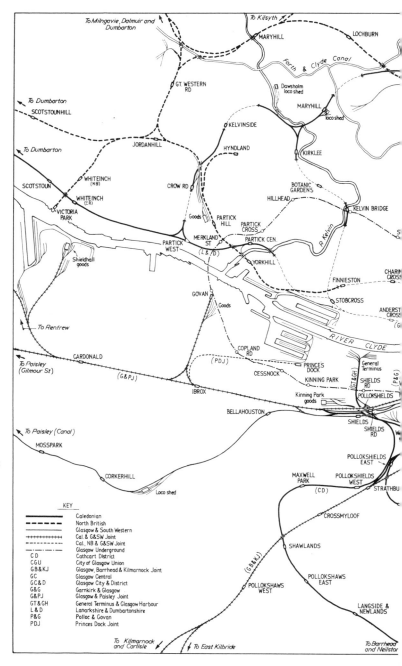

Fig 1    Map showing railways in the central area of Glasgow,

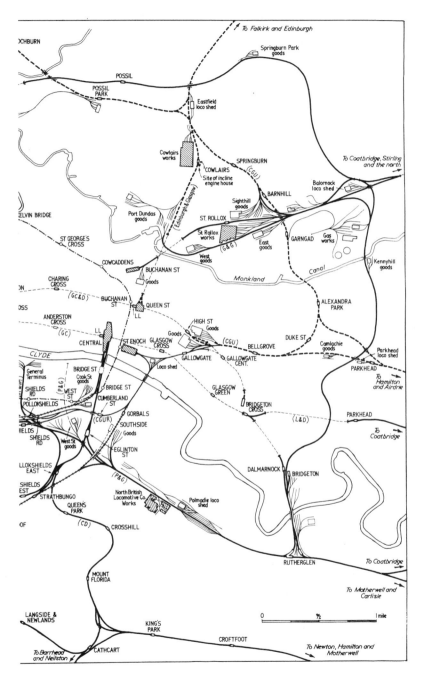

OCHBURN

To Falkirk and Edinburgh

POSSIL

Springburn Park goods

POSSIL PARK

Eastfield loco shed

Cowlairs works

COWLAIRS
Site of incline engine house

SPRINGBURN

(CGU)

BARNHILL

Balornock loco shed

To Coatbridge, Stirling and the north

Port Dundas goods

Sighthill goods

ST. ROLLOX

St Rollox works

(G&G)

East goods

GARNGAD

Gas works

KELVIN BRIDGE

ST GEORGE'S CROSS

West goods

Kennyhill goods

COWCADDENS

BUCHANAN ST

Goods

Monkland

Canal

CHARING CROSS

ON

(GC&D)

BUCHANAN ST

QUEEN ST

ALEXANDRA PARK

OSS

LL

ANDERSTON CROSS

(GC)

LL

High ST Goods

CENTRAL

ST ENOCH

GLASGOW CROSS

(CGU)

DUKE ST

BELLGROVE

Camlachie goods

Parkhead loco shed

CLYDE

GALLOWGATE

Loco shed

GALLOWGATE CENT.

PARKHEAD

To Hamilton and Airdrie

General Terminus

BRIDGE ST
Cook St goods

(P&G)

WEST ST

BRIDGE ST

GLASGOW GREEN

BRIDGETON CROSS

PARKHEAD

SHIELDS RD

POLLOKSHIELDS

CUMBERLAND ST

(L&D)

To Coatbridge

SHIELDS

(CGUR)

GORBALS

SOUTHSIDE

Goods

SHIELDS RD

West St goods

EGLINTON ST

DALMARNOCK

BRIDGETON

LLOKSHIELDS EAST

(P&G)

SHIELDS EST

STRATHBUNGO

North British Locomotive Co. Works

QUEEN'S PARK

Polmadie loco shed

To Coatbridge

OF

(CD)

CROSSHILL

RUTHERGLEN

To Motherwell and Carlisle

MOUNT FLORIDA

LANGSIDE & NEWLANDS

KING'S PARK

0    ½    1 mile

CROFTFOOT

To Newton, Hamilton and Motherwell

To Barrhead and Neilston

CATHCART

with original owning companies.

# INTRODUCTION

When Glasgow celebrated its 800th anniversary in May 1975, it was not mere coincidence that British Rail should hold an open day at its St Rollox workshops and Charles Street research laboratories—it was yet another reminder that whatever its social and economic problems the city is still the railway capital of Scotland. To those south of the Border, the real Scottish metropolis is always Glasgow, and a glance at a railway map shows why. Its position as the lowest bridging point on the Clyde has long made it a focus for communications, reflected in its functions as a cathedral and university city, and in its old-established rôle as a trading centre. After about 1780 it became a very successful manufacturing city, leading the west of Scotland, Britain and even the world in cotton manufacture, heavy engineering and shipbuilding. As early as 1855 *The Builder* was calling it 'the most go-ahead city in Great Britain', and by 1871, when the population was nearly half a million, it was being referred to as the second city of the British Empire.

The impact of Glasgow on foreign visitors was—then as now—immediate. One party of American tourists who had been guests of the Glasgow & South Western Railway (G&SW) in 1881 commented:

We are greatly surprised in Glasgow for she is a much larger and finer city than we expected to see; and your St Enoch Hotel far exceeds our expectations, not only in size, but in all her admirable appointments. Her table is one of the best we have ever patronised, and her dinners greatly excel anything we have met on this side of the Atlantic. Your shipbuilding on the Clyde is simply enormous. . . . Take it all and all, we

6

have met surprises all along our route; and we shall return to America with more exalted opinions of your people and of your industrial and commercial importance among the nations.

Today, most of the great ironworks and shipyards have gone, yet Glasgow is very much Scotland's premier commercial and shopping centre, the focal point of the great west of Scotland population belt. 'Progress' is still here, but as one traveller found in 1850, it is not necessarily a paradise:

The stranger entering Glasgow by any of its openings is not impressed with any very dignified notion of its grandeur and importance. By the Edinburgh and Glasgow and the Caledonian railways, on the north side of the Clyde, the approach is through tunnels; and on the south side the Glasgow and South Western and the Greenock railways conduct their passengers to the station along a line of ugly arches and over or through an inferior class of houses . . . Anon, as he enters the outskirts, his ear is dinned by the whirring of spindles, the noisy motion of power loom machinery, the brattling of hammers; and everything assures him that he is approaching one of the busiest haunts of mankind, and in a locality of which it may be truly said:

'Here Industry and Gain their vigils keep,
Command the Winds and tame the unwilling deep.'

Now it is the vast yet very lively and friendly Central Station which greets those Londoners who have come by the west coast route. Central is not only British Rail at its best, but is the greatest living monument to the Caledonian Railway. Affectionately nicknamed 'the Caley', its greatest rivals were the Glasgow & South Western—the G&SW—and the North British (NB). The last, with its Forth and Tay bridge routes, was the largest undertaking, but at Queen Street Station (Chapter 4) the problems seemed insoluble. The NB was more at home in

7

Edinburgh, the 'official' and administrative capital of Scotland whose Georgian elegance and white-collar economy have never been friends of the railway. Still, it was the headquarters of the NB, but as W. N. Acworth noted in 1890, although 'Edinburgh often boasts its superiority to Glasgow, in one respect at least—its railway stations—it must acknowledge its vast and apparently hopeless inferiority. The Caledonian Station is a wooden shanty. As for Waverley [the NB station], what pen could do justice to it?' By 1909 Waverley had been turned into the largest glass-covered area in Europe, yet in 1970 it was only handling 35,000 passengers per day, small indeed compared to the 100,000 at Central.

Glasgow has always gone in for things in a big way. As J. R. Kellett points out in his *Railways and the Victorian City* it was the only city apart from London 'which required a Royal Commission to analyse the multiplicity of urban railway projects'. By 1900 7.6 per cent of the central zone was railway-owned; only Liverpool at 9.0 per cent could beat this. Nevertheless, Glasgow is the winner when we come to bitter railway rivalries of which the 'battle of the railings and the arches' (Chapter 1) was only the most absurd of many. The end product was a fascinating duplication of services and the absence of a true joint terminal. In the 1880s the Caley and the NB went to war underground. Until 1964 one could travel on the CR Central Low Level branch, the last fully operational steam-hauled underground in Europe, aptly dubbed by Mr Hamilton Ellis as 'Sombre, sulphurous and Plutonian'.

Buchanan Street, once described as a 'country station in the city', was to the English visitor the most Scottish of the Glasgow terminals. Although a slum terminal, it was still the 'gateway to the Highlands' and in the early 1960s was the last haunt in Britain of the Gresley A4 Pacifics. Like Buchanan Street, St Enoch fell a victim to Beeching rationalisation. The only true rival to Central, it was 'in the Gothic style with mouldings of the early English period' and at the foot of its carriageway was an enamel advertisement informing all that

They come as a boon and a blessing to men
the Pickwick, the Owl, and the Waverley Pen.

Steel nibs rarely scratch Glaswegian ledgers today but until recently Queen Victoria was still on the move—underground! Now a municipal undertaking, the Glasgow Subway consists of 6¼ miles of 4ft 0in gauge track in two concentric circles; there are 15 stations with island platforms serving the north and south sides of the city centre.

The ticket office in St Enoch Square was housed in what can only be called a miniature Rhineland castle, but the fantasy was soon over, for after some narrow grimy stairs you were on an island platform standing before a 'Q Here' sign painted in white on the ancient concrete paving. Suddenly a train crawled in, a diminutive red affair, but only when you were on the move did you know why it had to crawl. While the conductor guard punched your tickets (at the end of the journey he collected these and deposited them in the box under the wooden stool in his compartment) cracked mahogany panels vibrated beneath a lining of formica and windows visibly moved in their frames. It was a miracle how this 1896 rolling stock held together, and the true connoisseur (if not choking to death in a smoking compartment, though the line was never steam-hauled) could spot a 1930 light bulb holder, a 1920 match striker, a 1950 chrome handle, and if he was lucky, a Victorian brass one. The subway was a service with that truly pre-war labour intensive flavour, but following the report of the Greater Glasgow Transport Executive (December 1973) it is slowly but surely being modernised. It will have escalators, a public address system, automatic ticketing and will act as an interchange link with bus, rail and private transport. The 1896 rolling stock has gone and those temperamental 40-year-old power cables will go. The Rhineland castle (which is a listed building) will be restored and rebuilt at a cost exceeding £100,000. Yet to those who have never enjoyed this ride into the past there is the consolation that a film has been made of the old lady, warts and

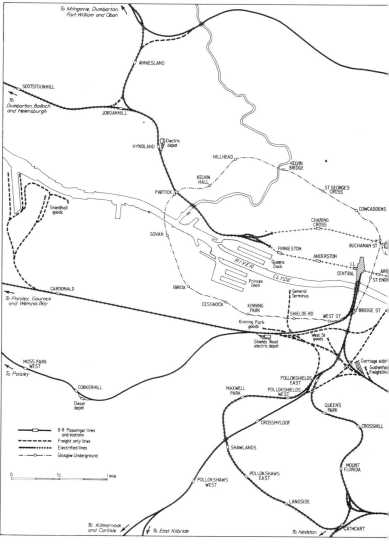

To Milngavie, Dumbarton,
Fort William and Oban

ANNIESLAND

SCOTSTOUNHILL

To
Dumbarton, Balloch
and Helensburgh

JORDANHILL

HYNDLAND — Electric depot

HILLHEAD

KELVIN BRIDGE

KELVIN HALL

PARTICK

ST GEORGE'S CROSS

Shieldhall goods

COWCADDENS

GOVAN

CHARING CROSS

FINNIESTON

BUCHANAN ST

ANDERSTON

Queens Dock

CARDONALD

IBROX

Princes Dock

CENTRAL

ARG
ST ENO

To Paisley, Gourock
and Wemyss Bay

CESSNOCK

KINNING PARK

General Terminus

SHIELDS RD

WEST ST

BRIDGE ST

Kinning Park goods

Shields Road electric depot

West St goods

MOSS PARK WEST

Carriage sidir
Gushetfa
Freight lin

To Paisley

CORKERHILL

POLLOKSHIELDS EAST

POLLOKSHIELDS WEST

MAXWELL PARK

Diesel depot

QUEENS PARK

CROSSMYLOOF

CROSSHILL

SHAWLANDS

MOUNT FLORIDA

——o—— B R Passenger lines
            and stations
- - - - - Freight only lines
+++++++ Electrified lines
—·—o—·— Glasgow Underground

0        ½           1 mile

POLLOKSHAWS WEST

POLLOKSHAWS EAST

LANGSIDE

To Kilmarnock
and Carlisle

To East Kilbride

To Neilston

CATHCART

Fig 2    Map of Glasgow railways today.

all. Still, the greatest event has been the electrification of the
main line between Glasgow and Crewe, in celebration of which
a full scale model of a Class 87 5000hp electric locomotive took
up station on the River Clyde between 22 April and 7 May
1974. Now the fastest time to London is five hours. When the

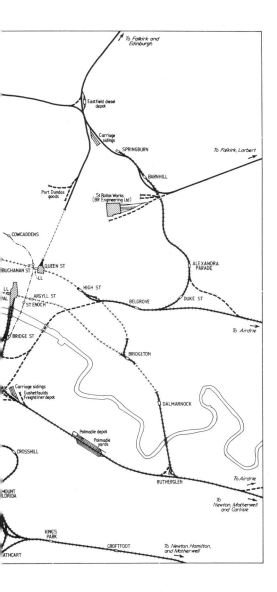

subway is fully modernised, no doubt for a day or two, there will be a mock-up of a train flying above the city.

Although Lenzie in 1850 was 'a perfect colony of Glasgow merchants', most of the population lived in tenements near the city centre which too often were 'executed by the amateur casual'. The density, in persons per acre, rose from 50 in 1841 to 94 in 1871, and there was correspondingly little growth in suburban traffic. When industry moved out of the city centre, for example to Govan, Scotstoun and Clydebank, new houses were commonly built nearby. Only in the 1880s with the opening of the Glasgow City and District Railway did workers' trains become important, linking the densely-populated east end of the area with the new shipyards and engineering works in the west. Although Clydebank suffered serious air raids, the rest of the city escaped lightly, so that until the late 1950s Glasgow was to all intents and purposes an intact Victorian metropolis. In 1876 a visitor noted that 'window gardening which has done so much to elevate the taste and feelings of the poor in the low quarters of London of late years is an occult science in Glasgow'. The huge redevelopment schemes of the 1960s gave comfortable and healthy houses on the outskirts, but where there should have been window boxes there are now wastelands, humming motorways, and above all loss of a sense of community. All too often one encounters small but very vociferous groups of the 'I belong to Glasgow' fraternity staggering to Queen Street and Central late at night. The one sobering thought is that they will be using a network of suburban railways second to none in Britain outside London. To redevelop and survive, Glasgow must continue to be a railway city, but the first electrification scheme nearly short-circuited itself out of existence.

The terminal of one's choice is clearly a highly personal matter. If you are an 'NB man', will never accept the amalgamations of 1923, and live in Edinburgh, then you will want the 'fairy palace' (Chapter 4) in George Square. If you are uncommitted (as most strangers are) then Central Station for its sheer effectiveness in modern conditions will have the appeal. Besides, it is the busiest passenger terminal in the UK, and offers a regular service on the Cathcart circle line to Pollokshaws East, right beside that superb museum of transport managed by Glasgow City Museums.

# 1

# TWO EARLY TERMINALS

## Townhead

An early writer in *The Railway Times* warned the proprietors of railways in the north of the temptation of 'squandering the funds of their constituents on ostentatious buildings'—he would have been pleased with the austere Townhead terminus of the Garnkirk & Glasgow Railway in Glebe Street. This was sketched by David Octavius Hill in one of his celebrated *Views of the Garnkirk & Glasgow Railway*, reproduced in John Thomas's *Regional History* (Vol. 6). From this it is clear that the terminus was designed primarily for coal traffic, with staithes for loading carts for land-sale, and loading points for transhipment of coal to canal barges.

One of the disadvantages of Glebe Street in the early days was that would-be passengers and carters on the direct road from Glasgow had to pass the toll gate of the Inchbelly Road Trust in Parliamentary Road, which could only be avoided by a lengthy detour on the Keppochill Road. In 1829 the Inchbelly trustees had failed to obtain extended powers from Parliament, yet in May 1830 they were attempting to levy tolls on the carts of Gourlay & Company, distillers, who regularly shipped their liquor by rail. The outcome was a compromise, the railway paying a lump sum of £100 a year. In 1839, the whole issue was fought out in the Court of Session, the first recognisable station litigation in Glasgow, but by no means the last.

Glebe Street was in any case inconveniently far from the city centre, though in its annual report for 1835 the company stated that 'perseverance in frequently advertising the passenger carriages of newspaper notices and otherwise is found to promote an increase of trade'. In 1832 the line had carried 62,605 passengers; by 1840 the annual total was just over 116,000. With the opening of the Slamannan Railway in August 1840, a connection was established with Causewayend, near Linlithgow, from which passengers could travel to Edinburgh by Union Canal boats or by stage coach.

Francis Whishaw describing Glebe Street commented in 1842 that 'at the St Rollox depot [ie Glebe Street] there are several lines of way; the buildings for the repairs of the locomotive engines, etc are here situate; and there is a small booking office and passenger hall, or what in England is better known as a waiting room'. This was almost certainly not the tiny stone bothy described as the first booking office and illustrated in articles and publicity about the Caledonian Railway from about 1900, particularly as during its demolition in the mid-1960s it was found to be built of stone sleepers discarded when the line was relaid, probably when it was re-gauged in the 1840s.

The first Caledonian Railway trains from the south terminated at Glebe Street (see Chapter 5) as did the company's Edinburgh service. However, the terminus was totally inadequate even for the Garnkirk & Glasgow by the mid-1840s when the company, by then the Glasgow, Garnkirk & Coatbridge, planned what became the CR Buchanan Street station. On the opening of Buchanan Street on 1 November 1849 Glebe Street ceased to be used for passengers (see Chapter 5), though as the 'St Rollox Depot' it remained an important mineral yard, continuing in use to a limited extent until about 1965 (Plate 1).

## Bridge Street Station

Glasgow's first true passenger terminal was in Bridge Street on the south bank. Its proximity to Glasgow Bridge made it a magnet for passengers. The station façade was an architectural masterpiece, and the travelling public had to wait over 30 years to see anything which could rival it. Bridge Street was a romantic product of the railway optimism of the early 1840s. Until February 1892 it was a joint station run by the Glasgow &

Paisley Joint Line Committee, a company jointly chaired by the GPK&A and the GP&G. All three companies were formed in 1837, but by 1850 the GPK&A was part of the G&SW and the GP&G had been absorbed by the Caledonian. The romantic optimism was then eclipsed by the battle of the companies. Furthermore, just getting to Bridge Street had involved an engineering feat well described in *The Railway Times* for 4 July 1840:

The railway is carried over four streets by centre arches of 46 feet span [14m], with side passages. Over King Street by a bridge of stone, and over Nelson Street, Wallace Street and Cook Street by bridges of iron. In addition to these, it is carried over 49 arches of brick [over 5 million bricks were used] of about 26 feet [7.8m] span; all of these in a distance of about 550 yards [504m]. Had the terminus been at Cook Street, the saving in property and building would have been great. The expense however will be in some degree compensated by the cellarage which so many arches afford.

The engineers to the Joint Line were Locke and Errington but it was John Miller who planned the layout of the station. Departing trains were to have 'two lines of way' and arriving trains three lines. Since the station was above street level 'there will be two main entrances from Bridge Street, from each of which there will be an easy stair leading to a long gallery on the level of the rails or nearly so, from the long gallery the three offices will have separate entrances'. If the basement is included, there were three floors, and as can be seen from Figs 3 and 4, the result was a building basically U-shape in plan. Miller foresaw that the terminal would outgrow itself. A Methodist chapel and houses were demolished to give 14,000 sq yd (11,600m²) for the depot, with 1½ acres (0.61 ha) between Paisley Canal and Cook Street 'kept in reserve for yards, stores and other necessary purposes'. In September 1841 it was found that the ground alone had cost over £25,000.

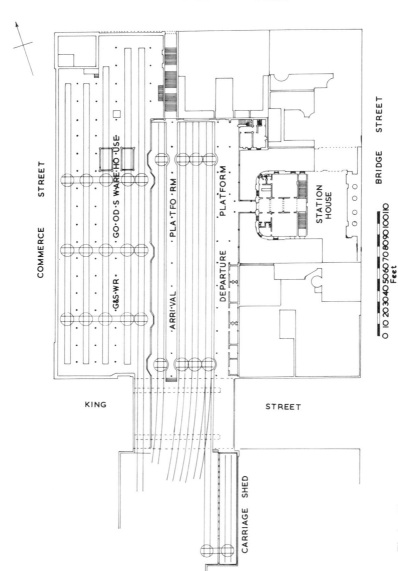

Fig 3   Plan of Bridge Street Station in 1851. Note the number of turntables in both goods and passenger stations. These were used for transferring 4-wheeled rolling stock from track to track.

16

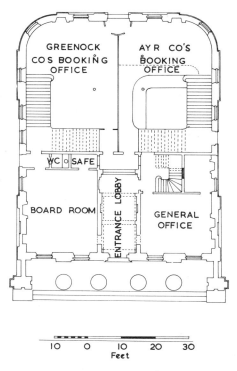

Fig 4    Plan of ground floor of 'Station House', Bridge Street, in 1844.

The permanent buildings were opened on 6 April 1841. The façade to Bridge Street was a superb portico surmounted by an entablature and pediment, and supported by four Doric columns 30ft 0in (9.1m) high. Errington it appears was much impressed by the new classical Glasgow Exchange, and in December 1839 had asked James Collie to prepare the designs. Collie believed the station would cost £3800, but two years later the final bill was well in excess of £7000 and included £716–5–6½ (£716.28) for the portico. The cost was shared as follows:

| | | |
|---|---|---|
| Joint Line | £3,697–0–0 | (£3,697.00) |
| Ayrshire Company | £2,863–13–8 | (£2,863.68) |
| Greenock Company | £920–18–6 | (£920.93) |

The station, a contemporary declared, afforded 'a striking display of the scientific skill of the architect, and shows on the other hand how very liberal in a pecuniary point of view, the Directors were disposed to act, when a great national undertaking was to be accomplished'. In fact this £7000 included the cost of a temporary structure which in July 1840 comprised a 'substantially built wooden booth covered with lead which is to be used for giving out tickets'. On 10 September 1840, in the presence of the Joint Committee, Collie had the pleasure of seeing the foundation stone of his building laid together with 'a memorial plaque, along with a vase hermetically sealed and containing copies of the Acts of Incorporation of the GPK&A and GPG and of the various newspapers of the city'. The contractor, John Buchanan, had begun work, promising to complete the job for £3995 if it was done in Kenmore stone, but stating that he would charge £950 extra if Humbie stone were used. On 6 February 1840 the Committee had definitely decided on 'the Doric elevation' but could just not make up its mind as to the interior arrangements of the building. If this was an example of company rivalries coming dangerously to the boil, it was nothing to what happened elsewhere. Joseph Locke suggested that ground south-east of the line adjoining Cook Street be used for engine sheds, each to be clearly demarcated by a wall. In September 1841 (by which time Locke had resigned) the Joint Committee was still squabbling as to who should have what.

## The Station in Operation

With the opening of Bridge Street, Glasgow was now placed within 24 hours' travel of London. In 1840 the companies had acquired a steamer called *Fire King*, which thrice a week plied between Ardrossan and Liverpool. Trains left Glasgow at 4.00pm arriving at Ardrossan at 6.00pm. Passengers then faced 13 hours at sea followed by a nine-hour journey by rail to the metropolis. Were station staff able to cope with the transportation revolution? At the Glasgow side of the business they were, judging by the remarkable Joint Line minute of 28 May 1840:

### GLASGOW STATION. ONE SUPERINTENDENT AND MASTER OF PORTERS

Should be a man of some experience in railways. Must have full authority over the servants of both companies and see that order is kept in the station—that every train starts to its time that arrival carriages are immediately cleaned and placed on departure rails—sufficient carriages must be brought up each morning and delivered clean and in perfect order to the superintendent by the servants of the respective companies. Should be entitled in cases of emergency to add on a carriage belonging to either company and generally have a discretionary power to make such arrangements as will always keep the station free and the trains to their time. Must report only to the joint committee, salary, say £130 a year.

### PORTERS

Three in station, two in office. Duties will consist in loading and unloading passenger luggage, cleaning the carriages, turning them, greasing the wheels. Running down an extra carriage, and if well behaved will be promoted pointsmen as vacancies occur. To be furnished with an undress uniform. Salary say 12 shillings a week.

### POINTSMEN

Two. Must have had some experience in points and crossings, can be called on by the superintendent for general duty, will be furnished with a police uniform. Salary say 15 shillings a week.

## POLICEMEN

One in station, one in office, one at Moss Road. The two former to keep order in the station and office, to assist the superintendent and to carry orders. Salary 15 shillings a week.

## COKE AND WATERMEN

Two. Available for any duty if called on by the superintendent. Salary 12 shillings a week.

A minute of 4 June 1840 decreed that 'pointsmen were to be named by Mr Errington and liable to instant dismissal in case of misbehaviour or neglect'. The first station master was also appointed by Errington, 'no suitable agent being found'. The porters lodged in rooms in the station, but in 1843 the Joint Line Committee thought of moving them out since it might give relief 'from the payment of the window tax'. Some early 2–2–2 locomotives for the GPK&A were designed by John Miller, one of them, *Lightning*, being built at Cook Street in 1846. However, at this period most companies continued to order their locomotives from private firms. Moreover the GPK&A was far more interested in just keeping its trains on the rails. In December 1840 the GPK&A's train from Paisley ran out of steam 30yd beyond Shields Bridge and avoided colliding with another 'within a hair's breadth'. On 24 January 1867 a train from Greenock left the rails near Cook Street and 'fell fifteen feet into Messrs Miller & Company's asphalt works—there were about thirty passengers in the carriage most of whom were more or less injured but no one fatally'. Until 1843 (when movable platforms were installed) passengers used badly-designed steps to leave and enter carriages. At least first-class passengers could look at a newspaper 'left daily in the waiting room', although this was often stolen by the porters. By 1846 the station had two newsvendors, one a retired porter. In 1847 the pressure of rapidly increasing goods traffic, had forced the GPK&A to build a range of warehouses in

Commerce Street (Fig 3). Various minor alterations were also made to the passenger station by the Joint Line including a much called for 'separate and distinct entrance for the third class passengers' (Plate 2).

The desire for segregation of working-class passengers stemmed from a deliberate policy decision on the part of the directors of the Greenock line. In 1844 *Hansard* reported that the fares on that line were only 2s 3d (12p) per 100 miles (161km), much lower than on any English or Irish lines, and that 'the Company found that the conveyance [of third-class passengers] was attended with so little expense that they expressed their pleasure that it was in their power to do a great amount of good, while they were obtaining a return for their capital'. The company was, at the time, engaged in direct competition with established river steamer services.

A plan by the Glasgow architect and engineer Hugh Maclure (Fig 3) shows Bridge Street in 1851 with four lines and eight turnplates, and an arrival platform 840ft 0in × 10ft 0in (256.0m × 3.0m). A departure platform of the same length faced the station buildings, giving a primitive concourse 428ft 0in × 20ft 0in (130.0m × 6.0m) whose area is increased if we include the curious L-shaped entrance on each of the longer sides of the building. The goods station adjacent to Commerce Street had six lines with fifteen turnplates. There was also a long range of G&SW goods warehouses linked to street level by two hoists. Compared with Queen Street Station, this layout is less confused. However, the Royal Commission which sat in Glasgow in 1847 found that whereas Queen Street occupied 3.5 acres (1.42ha), Bridge Street only covered 0.75 acre (0.3ha) yet was handling over 1 million passengers. Much of this was short-distance traffic to and from Paisley, Barrhead, Thornliebank and Greenock. Between 1855 and 1879 the engineers made many minor improvements to the station, though its geographical position made physical expansion difficult.

The refreshment rooms had a chequered history. Let to a

Miss Reid in 1855 (who was also responsible for cleaning part of the station) they were discontinued on 25 March 1858 and converted into waiting rooms. By 1870 refreshments were again in evidence. Miss Reid offered a rent of £200, but was outbid by a Mr Conacher who had offered £10 more. On 6 June 1890 it was reported that the rent had been reduced to £25, but that the rooms were now closed 'owing to want of traffic'. Although MacFarlane's cast-iron urinals had been first installed in July 1856, in the following year the Lord Justice Clerk wrote bitterly to the Joint Line of the 'insanitary sanitary accommodation'. As if to pacify him, the company had the station platforms asphalted. But the gadget adopted on 30 January 1874 was perhaps the solution to the problem (a self-acting register intended to show the number of persons using the water closets—a charge of one penny for each person using them). Between 1857 and 1861 Hugh Maclure improved the station lighting by introducing plate-glass windows and a glass roof at each side of the grand colonnade. The side walls of the old booking office were removed, and replaced by columns. The company appointed a new station master in 1858, but he was soon sacked for incompetence and replaced by Mr James Edgar 'conductor upon the Glasgow & London Mail Trains'.

In comparison to the schemes put forward by William Johnstone and George Graham these were trivial changes. In 1862 they planned to increase the arching accommodation—but quickly abandoned this when they realised it would cost not less than £1,150. Realising that the recently-opened Wemyss Bay and Bridge of Weir lines were producing increasing numbers of passengers, in September 1863 they reported on the necessity of acquiring the whole properties between Eglinton Street and Commerce Street on the east and west, and between King Street and Cook Street on the north and south. The company thought otherwise, and sanctioned instead a small bothy at the west end of the departure platform for supplying hot water for carriage warming-pans. By 1866 officials were uncertain as to whether or not Bridge Street would still be used for passengers in ten years' time, and by 1870 it was recognised that the opening of the new station at St Enoch Square (Chapter 3) was the real solution. Unfortunately by that time valuable property had been acquired for Bridge Street improvements, but when pressed by the Caledonian, the G&SW would not co-operate in any alterations, and suggested that the properties be let instead. The G&SW wanted first and foremost to get to St Enoch, and keep the Caledonian out. However, in 1870 the Caledonian's most immediate worry was the agency which was creating St Enoch—the City of Glasgow Union Railway. By an agreement of 1838 (subsequently modified in 1855–8) traffic between Glasgow and Paisley was shared jointly, but through traffic passing over the Joint Line to and from places beyond Paisley was exempt from any toll. However, was all traffic of the G&SW passing from the CGU to stations on the Joint Line through traffic or not? In its report of 12 September 1871 the Joint Line Committee suggested that the squabbles could only be solved if through traffic distinctions were abolished, and the companies charged equally as on the Kilmarnock Joint Line, but it was pointed out that this had required an Act of Parliament. In 1873 there was a serious collision at Bridge Street due, claimed the Board of Trade, to 'the traffic having outgrown the capabilities of the station'. The companies then reconsidered their schemes of 1866, but in the event it was the Caledonian which had to foot the bill for the construction of the new Bridge Street Station, having to make this concession to the G&SW if it was to build its grand Central Station in Gordon Street (Chapter 2). In 1870, with the prospect of St Enoch Station still distant, the G&SW secretly recognised little long-term advantage in an enlarged Bridge Street. In rebuilding Bridge Street the Caledonian was not faced with more than the usual engineering problems, and the land for enlargement had been given free by the G&SW. Nevertheless, the scene was set for one of the most notorious 'confrontations' in Glasgow's railway history.

*The Battle of the Railings and the Arches 1876–1882*

With the opening of Dunlop Street, the stepping stone to St Enoch (Chapter 3), Bridge Street was only used by G&SW local trains. From 1 July 1879 to 1 August 1879 Central Station was still not complete, so that Bridge Street was used for Caledonian trains to and from East Kilbride, Busby, Motherwell, Hamilton and Strathaven, services previously terminating at Southside and Gorbals. The through lines to Central Station were to the east—they had two platforms which could be reached by an additional entrance in Clyde Place. The dock platforms were moved westwards, two being reserved for the Caledonian, the other pair for the G&SW. Section 26 of the Caledonian Railway (Gordon Street Station Connecting Lines) Act 1875 had said that should the two companies disagree as to the remodelling, an arbiter would be appointed by the Board of Trade. It was T. E. Harrison who was given the thankless task of sorting out the differences between George Cunningham (the Caley's consulting engineer) and Andrew Galloway of the G&SW yet at a meeting in London in April 1876 it turned out that the problems were short-lived, and both parties cheerfully made concessions. Galloway's plans showed a thin blue line dividing the station—what was it? Under cross-examination he was later to admit that to the engineer such a line might represent anything. As it turned out it became a wall, later modified to a railing, which if erected would force Caledonian passengers changing at Bridge Street for Wemyss Bay trains on the Joint Line to go downstairs and out to Clyde Place and then come up again. This 400yd (366m) detour would have to be made in not more than ten minutes during the busy summer months, otherwise the Wemyss Bay connection would be lost. Between 12 February 1876 and 26 February 1880 240 vitriolic letters and telegrams had passed between the contenders. Harrison believed that 'whatever is done should be designed to give as much convenience to the public as possible'. He was tired of being a pawn in the battle of the companies, but Andrew Galloway was not. On 19 October 1876, judging by the following letter to Cunningham, he was not interested in the legal niceties which were the crux of the matter:

I have always disputed the right of the Caledonian Company to use the Joint Line Offices and accommodation for their traffic using the Gordon Street Station lines, and you were aware of this when the plan was agreed to.

Galloway's attack began on the width between Commerce Street and the centre line of the Caledonian. Cunningham, he said, had altered his measurements at the G&SW's expense. Then while Harrison made conciliating moves he questioned the designs for the bridge carrying the CGU over Wallace Street, ignoring the fact that the necessary negotiations (required under section 46 of the 1875 Act) had been successfully concluded. Cunningham lost his temper and wrote to W. J. Wainwright, the G&SW general manager, suggesting that while it was G&SW policy not to have WCs off the gentlemen's waiting rooms, Galloway had made secret plans of his own which if carried out would have to be changed by demolition. If this really was a possibility, Galloway remained suspiciously quiet. At least Cunningham drew from Wainwright the assurance that 'the question of WC's or no WC's in the gentlemen's waiting rooms . . . cannot affect the general plan of the station', but the engineering department of the G&SW was still in fighting spirit. On 8 November 1877 the Caledonian were told that the stair tower at the south-west corner of the new train shed was not what had been agreed, and construction was held up until December. Even the room for foot warmers left much to be desired for it had been contracted from a width 15ft 0in (4.6m) to a width of only 14ft 2in (4.3m). In the vicinity of the canal the Caledonian was on a stickier wicket, for the temporary stopping-up of streets and the leaking of a coffer dam caused inevitable inconvenience, but stories of police 'complaints' about Salkeld Street only reached officials via Andrew Galloway on 22 November 1879.

Cunningham refused to reconsider the G&SW demands for a dividing railing, and on 7 December 1881 the Court of Session decided in favour of the Caledonian. In his summing-up, Lord Rutherfurd Clark found no evidence of a legally binding agreement. Galloway, he said, had spoken with 'the most perfect honesty' but did not recommend himself 'as an accurate or reliable witness'.

In extending the station westward to Commerce Street the Caledonian acquired land free of charge (and without trouble) from the Joint Committee. This necessitated a continuation of the arches, but the plans were modified so that the train shed could be extended further southwards, and it was agreed that in the frontage of Commerce Street, the arches should be formed into shops. However, in doing this the Caledonian acquired land from third parties for £3000. The shops cost £25,000 to build, but were they not a Caledonian investment on Caledonian land as at Carlisle Citadel where the LNWR owned the line above and the solum of the arches belonged to the Caledonian? Andrew Galloway thought otherwise: at Bridge Street, he said, all the arches were joint property. In the witness box he painted a gloomy picture of eroding brickwork and the likelihood of the shops being used for purely railway purposes but escaping Joint Line control, but when questioned by counsel as to their ownership, he replied 'I cannot speak exactly upon that'. The court thought otherwise and ruled that the G&SW was not entitled to share rents and profits, and awarded £170 legal costs against the company.

## A Pyrrhic Victory

The whole episode was really a Pyrrhic victory for the Caledonian, the works for the new station had cost £150,000, only £40,000 less than their first Central Station (Chapter 2). The roof of the reconstructed Bridge Street (Plate 5) consisted of transverse parallel lattice girders, 12ft 0in (3.66m) deep and 31ft 6in (9.6m) apart with uncovered spaces to minimise the corrosive effects of engine blast. The roof of the first Central Station was a larger version of the same thing—Cunningham Blyth and Westland being always reluctant to experiment with iron arches of large span. Just before the G&SW relinquished ownership in 1892, improvements to Central Station had necessitated a widening of Bridge Street and an extension of its façade to the designs of James Miller. Part of the buildings were damaged by fire, but it was the drastic modernisation of Central Station in 1904 which was the death blow. The old roof realised £575–17–6 (£575.87½) scrap value, and on 6 February 1905 the railway decided to convert the remaining buildings into shops and houses. Miller's façade still survives, but Collie's was badly mutilated in the 1950s and finally demolished in 1971. George Cunningham once described the terminal as 'a place like a church with large columns in front'. It was certainly a Euston-type hymn to the iron horse, but it gave birth to no classical offspring. The inter-company rivalries and financial uncertainties after 1840 soon made sure of that.

# 2

# CENTRAL STATION

If there is anything which manages to convey in miniature the bustle, size, and social variety of the City of Glasgow then it is Central Station. The commuter, the inter-city executive and the excursionist could not do without it but it would be wrong to say that any group receives preferential treatment. Should you wish to see the station at its busiest the best time is during the Glasgow Fair Holiday (12–15 July). In 1973 during the Fair more than 80 trains, not including an excellent service of local specials, left for various English destinations. Forty-three of these went to London. Indeed, Central is very special, for it is the busiest passenger terminal in the UK. For example, when St Enoch closed in 1966 it had to take another 250 trains and 23,000 passengers each day, and with the electrification of the Clyde Coast lines in the following year another 100 passenger services were added to the timetables. During an average weekday in November 1974 Central handled 82,598 passengers and 963 trains. Whatever the pressure, Central can take it; the foresight of its Edwardian designers, electrification, and the latest signalling technology are the keys to its success.

Without doubt it is the most exciting station in Glasgow, for it handles the Glasgow–London expresses. Of the day trains, the most famous is the Royal Scot, hauled in the 1950s by a Stanier Pacific. These and a host of other pre-war types made Central the mecca for the steam enthusiast. With the introduction of diesels in the 1960s the old magic vanished, yet the introduction on 6 May 1974 of a fleet of Class 87 5000hp electrics with fully air-conditioned coaches was more than just a revolution in comfort. When the West Coast route opened in 1848, London was nearly a day away. Part of the problem had been negotiating the severe gradients at Beattock, but now two of these Class 87s can easily move 1300 tons at 100mph, while the following figures show why the 'Electric Scots' are already part of the folklore of Central Station:

GLASGOW–EUSTON EXPRESSES

| Year | Fastest Time | Average Time | Number of trains each way per day |
|------|--------------|--------------|-----------------------------------|
| 1973 | 5hr 56min | 6hr 04min | 5 |
| 1974 | 5hr 0min | 5hr 12min | 8 |

These trains are served by platforms 1 and 2. In 1970 the first reception lounge for rail sleeper passengers in Britain was opened at platform 1. It bears a plaque unveiled by the Queen on 7 May 1974 'to mark the final stage of electrifying the railway from London to Glasgow'.

As in 1906, the most remarkable feature of Central is its concourse; a gigantic triangle on gently rising gradients whose angularity is broken by curvaceous brown varnished stalls and the Caledonian Restaurant. Above the last is one of the most remarkable pre-1914 train information indicators in Europe. Seventy-four feet long, it boasts a window (neatly numbered in white enamel) for each of the 13 platforms. The 'state of play' of any platform is shown by removing a panel from a library of destinations and fixing it to the appropriate window. Central no longer has waiting rooms, so it is not uncommon for the tired and the bored to become spectators of the indicator football match. Even the 7.30pm 'To London for Mails Only' served by platform 11 (where there are hoists to the mail depot in the basement) appears on the score.

Before World War I, during the summer months Central became alive with the boat train expresses ferrying holidaymakers to Gourock, Wemyss Bay and Ardrossan. At the height of the season the Caledonian might run 30 each way daily and to

29

make sure that passengers would embark promptly timetabled some with 'no luggage allowed'. Now, economic realities and changing holiday patterns have made 'going down the water' a shadow of what it once was. Even so, Ardrossan during the Glasgow Fair in 1973 was getting eleven specials for the Arran sailings. From May to September there is a fairly frequent service from Ardrossan to the Isle of Man. Although Messrs Burns and Laird Lines Ltd run steamers from Ardrossan to Belfast, the British Rail Stranraer–Larne route is the most regular, and by its very nature gives Central Station a 'continental' atmosphere which though not akin to that of Victoria is the nearest thing approaching it in the Scottish context.

Central has not escaped modernisation. In 1966 the 15in Beardmore Howitzer shell collecting box, for long the favourite meeting place of sweethearts, was moved from the centre of the booking hall to a new site near the left luggage office, but the delightful 15ft 0in high Victorian clock on the roof of the bookstall disappeared to make way for the present rather impersonal all-digit 24-hour affair. The new 'superloos' are a happier story. In the ladies especially no cost has been spared in creating a relaxing atmosphere, for as well as a nursing mothers' room there are 'fitted carpet, soft lights, tropical plants and flowers and music'. Canned music is also broadcast through the public address system. Drowned by the roar from daytime rush-hours, in the evening it takes its revenge on railway traditionalists by spewing forth all the latest 'hits'.

The new east side refreshment complex was completed in 1969 at a cost of £100,000 but compared with the establishment at Queen Street is rather a disappointment. Although the self-service cafeteria specialises in home baking and was the first public area in Britain to have non-skid rubber tiled flooring, the Caledonia Restaurant fits rather awkwardly into the old waiting room. The trouble is that unlike at Queen Street there is no George Square to gaze upon. Another impression is that the new facilities are not quite keeping pace with increasing demand. In the Royal Scot and Arran Lounge bars especially, 'standing room only' is the rule rather than the exception.

From the plush-carpeted Central Station Hotel a deliciously curved corner entrance leads you right on to the north-west end of the concourse, but the best pedestrian access (and it costs nothing) is the grand entrance in Gordon Street described in 1881 as having 'panelled pilasters with carved and fluted capitals carrying semi circular arches . . . protected by elaborate hammered iron grills by Skidmore of Coventry'.

Within, a battery of stainless-steel ticket windows has replaced the old wooden booking office, but outside there is still the original iron-and-glass portico bearing an ancient notice warning that 'vehicles must not wait here'.

The policy at Central is to keep the best of the old if it works. Thus between platforms 11 and 12 generous car parking is provided by the 30ft-wide carriageway completed in 1906; vehicles enter and leave by mysterious white-tiled tunnels in Hope Street. Central has the following platforms:

| Platform | Length in feet | Platform | Length in feet |
|----------|----------------|----------|----------------|
| 1 | 918 | 8 | 405 |
| 2 | 1020 | 9 | 940 |
| 3 | 610 | 10 | 913 |
| 4 | 572 | 11 | 1160 |
| 5 | 498 | 11a | 436 |
| 6 | 423 | 12 | 635 |
| 7 | 426 | 13 | 808 |

Numbers 9–13 actually extend to the bridge over the river, which only carries eight lines. A feature of the station is the disproportionately large volume of daytime local traffic. More trains go to Lanark, Shotts, Hamilton, Barrhead, Kilmarnock and Ayr than ever go to London. On Saturday mornings, the place is swamped by shoppers and it is a battle to get near any one of the ten ticket windows in Gordon Street. There are so

many trains, that throughout the working week recourse is had
to double-banking; two or even three trains may depart in suc-
cession from the same platform. Large pre-war housing
schemes have made the Cathcart Circle and the lines to Kirk-
hill and Neilston some of the busiest suburban routes outside
London. To ease congestion, these trains are usually worked
from platforms 6, 7 and 8, which are in line with the main exit.
A time-honoured Saturday function of this line is the ferrying
of myriads of football fans to Mount Florida Station which is
adjacent to Hampden Park Stadium. The operation goes like
clockwork, but entails a suspension of all ordinary traffic for
the more important matches.

Another fast and crowded service is on the 37-mile stretch to
Gourock, Greenock and Wemyss Bay. All-electric since 1967,
it is now controlled from the signalling centres at Central,
Gourock and Paisley in conjunction with lineside automatic
switching stations which enjoy the distinction of being the first
in the Glasgow area to be all-plastics prefabricated structures.
Like Glasgow, Greenock has been blitzed by redevelopment
so at Branchton, five miles from the city centre, there is an entirely new station serving the dormitory suburbs of Larkfield
and Pennyfern. In one week in 1968, Branchton's receipts rose
by nearly 1500 per cent. As might be expected, Glasgow is the
most popular venue, but in the evening there is a sizeable traffic to the public houses of Wemyss Bay. Unimaginative plan-
ners sought to keep Branchton 'dry' and the railway has
become the lifeline of the thirsty. The Wemyss Bay and other
Clyde Coast trains use platforms 10–13 in Central Station.

## Early History

The Caledonian Railway had originally intended to have its
main Glasgow station on almost the same site on which St
Enoch station was eventually built. This 'Dunlop Street Station' (see Fig 17) was planned by the Clydesdale Junction Railway, but owing to Admiralty objections to the original plans

32

*Plates 1 and 2. (Above)* The carriage shed at Glebe Street in 1966. The flat was occupied as a dwelling house. *(Below)* Bridge Street Station *circa* 1860. The separate entrance for 3rd class passengers is on the right. Note the sign directing passengers to the Electric Telegraph Office. [*John R. Hume; Strathclyde Regional Archives*]

*Plates 3 and 4. (Above)* The Commerce Street side of Bridge Street Station *circa* 1860, showing the train shed on the left. Note the vintage rolling stock and the early telegraph poles. *(Below)* Bridge Street Station in 1877, during the construction of the first Central Station. Part of the train shed has been demolished, showing the unusual roof trusses. [*Strathclyde Regional Archives; Blyth & Blyth*]

and to shortage of capital the project was abandoned (see Chapter 5). Opposition from the Clyde Trustees and the high cost of land in a prime commercial area effectively prevented development of a terminal on the north bank until the 1870s, though at the peak of the 1860s boom the Caley bought land at Blythswood Holm, to the west of the present Central Station, as part of an elaborate scheme to link existing lines on the south of the Clyde with new lines on the north bank.

A correspondent in *The Engineer* (5 January 1866) noted that 'the Caledonian Company is about to ask Parliament for power to raise £6,659,700 of new capital. This company proposes a great station in the heart of Glasgow at the cost of £2,000,000 with several miles of underground railway with viaducts over and tunnels under the Clyde and with suburban circuits of the most costly kind', but added that the Caley would not proceed with this scheme unless the other companies went ahead with competing projects.

The collapse of the boom relieved both the Caley and the North British from pursuing what were at the time ruinously expensive projects, and delayed completion of the City of Glasgow Union Railway's plans for a central station at St Enoch Square. One of the by-products of the prosperity of the mid-1860s was a series of amalgamations which greatly extended the capital base of the NB and Caledonian railways. When the next boom came in the early 1870s—and it was a remarkable one—the Caledonian was able to raise money to promote a Bill for an extension from Bridge Street to Gordon Street. The Caley was forced into this by the exorbitant rates proposed by the G&SW for access to its new station (Chapter 3).

In the Caledonian Railway (Gordon Street Glasgow Station) Act as passed in 1873 the Caledonian's plan was to widen the existing low-level road bridge over the Clyde at the Broomielaw and to carry a rail bridge over it on a series of columns, as in the High Level Bridge at Newcastle. For this concession it paid £22,500 in compensation to the Clyde Trustees, but the scheme had to be dropped when it was found that too much valuable frontage property would have to be acquired. Two years later the company obtained powers to construct the bridge 50yd (46m) downstream, for which it paid £73,000 for wayleave concessions. This sum included £25,000 to the Glasgow Bridges Trust for widening Thomas Telford's bridge at the Broomielaw, the task the railway had originally promised to do. The bridge was not in fact widened until the 1890s.

The rail bridge was designed by Blyth & Cunningham of Edinburgh, the contractors being William Arrol & Company of Glasgow. Work began in May 1876 and was completed on 1 October 1878 (see Plates 6, 8). The viaduct was 701ft 0in (213.7m) long, but because the engineer to the Clyde Trustees insisted that the piers must be in the line of those of the old road bridge, to aid navigation, there was a variation in the five spans. The first on the south bank was 61ft 0in (18.6m), the next 164ft 6in (50.1m), the centre one 186ft 0in (56.7m), the fourth 151ft 0in (46m), and that on the north side 89ft 0in (27.1m). The bridge was designed to carry four lines of rails 37ft 9in (11.5m) above high water at the spring tides, but over the streets and quays the headway was 20ft 0in (6.1m). The superstructure was of wrought-iron lattice girders resting on cast-iron cylinders filled with Portland cement concrete, and built up with courses of freestone and Dalbeattie granite. Cast-iron arches had to be placed for 'ornament' between each of the river piers. There was only one anxious moment during construction, and that occurred at the north quay when on the cracking of a neighbouring wall, digging inside a cylinder had to be abandoned. Messrs Arrol then loaded it with 500 tons (508 tonnes) of short rails and pig-iron, but nothing happened for several days until suddenly without warning it sank 20ft 0in (6.1m) yet remained truly vertical.

If the Clyde Trustees were difficult to please (the bridge alone cost £64,000) the Glasgow & South Western was even more so, for it insisted that not only should Bridge Street Station be preserved, but that it should be entirely rebuilt at Cale-

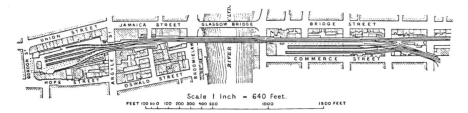

Fig 5 Plan of Central Station (Gordon Street Station) as first built, showing how the operation of the station was cramped by the existence of Bridge Street Station (*right*).

donian expense (see Chapter 1). As a partner in the Glasgow & Paisley Joint Line, it was prepared to grant the additional land required free, but early in December 1878 was inserting advertisements in the local press warning the public that building operations at Bridge Street had made train working liable to accident. In November 1878 W. J. Wainwright, general manager of the G&SW, complained that the Caledonian was acting in a 'high handed and illegal manner'. The battle of the railings and arches (Chapter 1) had begun in earnest. Furthermore, the original Central Station opened in December 1879 was small consolation for the £150,000 of Caledonian money spent on enlarging Bridge Street, for it quickly became congested. The eight platforms were short and narrow (some were only 14ft 0in (4.3m) wide), while there was no good cab stance nor adequate auxiliary sidings (Fig 5). Of the four approach lines on Clyde Bridge, one had to be used as a carriage siding. Completed in 1882, the booking hall was described as having a ceiling 'divided into 280 panels, which are filled in with enamelled iron plates, decorated in four colours, with a conventional design' but the circulating area (Plate 11, Fig 5) was ridiculously small. The one redeeming feature was its gradient of 1 in 18 from Gordon Street towards the platforms which had 'the effect of mitigating crushing in the vicinity of the ticket windows'. In 1899, 16,841,070 and 6,415,936 travellers used Central High and Low Levels respectively.

Low Level, on the Glasgow Central Railway, had been opened on 10 August 1896 (Plate 13, Fig 7). This expensive and at first nominally independent line was designed partly for suburban traffic, but also to give the Caledonian Railway direct access to Queen's Dock. Of its 7 miles (18.1km), 5 (13km) were underground, much of it only inches below Argyle Street, Trongate, London Road and other main streets. With connecting lines, a short-lived north side circular service was provided, together with trains to the west end, and stations on the north bank of the Clyde. The clientele of the line varied from businessmen from Kelvinside and Kirklee to artisans and labourers on the intensive shuttle from east-end stations to shipyards and engineering works down river. The low-level Central station could also be used for main line trains diverted at Rutherglen, and by a circuitous route as a terminus for south side suburban trains. There were two island platforms 600ft 0in × 30ft 0in (183.0m × 9.1m), and the station was lined with white tiles, with the steel girders painted pale green, and the supporting columns buff with dark green bases. The original intention was to have a separate entrance to the station, on the north-west corner of Hope Street and Argyle Street, and a temporary wooden office was erected (illustrated in John Thomas's *Regional History*). The permanent domed building planned by J. J. Burnet was not built, and in the extension of the main-line station after 1899 (see below) an entrance from within the new building was provided. On the abandoned site a single-storey range of shops was built in 1908.

## Central Station Hotel

The hotel, built of Dunmore stone, is in a Queen Anne style (Plates 9, 10), a dramatic departure from the heavy gothic of St Enoch. *The Builder* commented in 1898:

One hesitates a little to classify its style. At the time it was built it might have been called 'Queen Anne' but it is more restrained than most of the architecture that was then perpetrated in that Royal Lady's name—at any rate it

is thoroughly well adopted to the purpose of the building
. . . the tower alone does not appear quite a success.

It was designed by Rowand (later Sir Rowand) Anderson of
Edinburgh, who was also responsible for the furniture in the
public rooms. Seven storeys high (exclusive of basement) and
with nearly 400 rooms, the ridge of its roof is 116ft 0in (35.4m)
above street level. In 1974 British Rail, on grounds of fire
safety and greater efficiency, decided to close the St Enoch
Hotel and concentrate the hotel business at Central; BR probably owe a functional building more to Caledonian mismanage-
ment than to Victorian architectural foresight. Glaswegians
reading the *Glasgow Herald* on 25 October 1880 were aston-
ished to learn that the pile built to replace the Caledonian's
cramped offices at Buchanan Street was to become instead a
magnificent station hotel which 'should be opened next
summer'. Readers were assured that 'conversion under revised
plans may easily be accomplished', yet the completion of these
alterations was not celebrated until 27 June 1883 when a
supper was given at the hotel by Messrs Watt & Wilson to their
200 workmen. There was a touch of irony in Mr Watt's remark
that they were looking at 'one of the best built and finished
buildings in Europe', for what had been achieved had required
the demolition of a large amount of work already done (see
Plate 9). The 129ft 0in (39.3m) tower at the corner of Gordon
Street and Hope Street contained the main staircase and ele-
vator; it had once contained board rooms and offices. As at St
Enoch, kitchen premises were easily relegated to the basement.
The dining room was a different matter. In fitting it into a
corner over the cab approach in Hope Street the contractors
encountered numerous small offices divided by stone walls 2ft
6in (0.76m) thick. It was then found that the ceiling was too
low, and so the second floor above was pulled down as well.
The billiards room occupied a short entresol floor to the west of
a new booking hall in Gordon Street, much of the first floor
being cut away to provide adequate height to the concourse.

To minimise fire risk, the floors of the bedroom corridors were of concrete slabs laid on malleable iron joists. Traces of the office plan probably survived in the bedrooms for, by unlocking doors on either side, each room communicated with its neighbours. This it was claimed was 'for the convenience of a party who may wish to occupy several adjoining rooms'. The cost of these alterations was about £57,000, excluding fittings. The carpeting required amounted to 7200 sq yd (6581m²), there were 1200 electric bells, 5000ft (1524m) speaking tubes, and 29 miles (46.7km) of bell wire weighing 2.5 tons (2.6 tonnes). Incandescent electric lighting was installed in 1884 by Anderson & Munro, who agreed to light the public rooms at an annual cost of £434. The lighting installation was extended in 1885 by the Anglo-American Brush Electric Light Co, and again by Mavor & Coulson in 1890. The first manager, a Mr Lord, was appointed in March 1881, though the hotel did not open until 19 June 1885. His salary of £500 a year was supplemented by 5 per cent commission on drawings. His successor, a Mr Turnbull appointed in 1887, was less fortunate: he got £350 with board on the understanding that 'he shall not accept commissions or allowances by way of discounts or otherwise for furnishings or supplies to the hotel or refreshment rooms in any manner whatever'.

When the station was reconstructed in 1901–6, the hotel was also extended, to designs by James Miller, whose fee was the 'lump sum of £1350'. Somewhat similar in design to Rowand Anderson's part, the extension cost £179,793–12s–2d (£179,793.61) including 'fireproofing' at a price of £3000. A garage was incorporated, for the use of which Scottish Automobile Association members paid 1s–0d (5p) a day and others 1s–6d (7½p). The extension opened on 15 April 1907.

The hotel today is one of the most comfortable and up-to-date in Britain, and a glance at the British Transport Hotels brochures gives an idea of its size.

| Hotel | No of bedrooms | Maximum accommo- dation |
|---|---|---|
| Midland (Manchester) | 312 | 450 |
| Caledonian (Edinburgh) | 222 | 388 |
| Central (Glasgow) | 221 | 307 |
| Gleneagles (Perthshire) | 210 | 383 |
| Charing Cross (London) | 210 | 273 |

## Central Station in the Age of the Electric Scots

A ninth platform was added in 1889, but most of the 13-acre complex we know today dates from 1901–6. Essentially, this involved a widening to the west and a lengthening to the south (Figs 6 and 7). The second bridge over the Clyde, platforms 10–13, a vast underground service complex, the hydraulic buffer stops, the train information indicator, the 25 shops under Argyle Street Bridge and the concourse are the most tangible signs of this revolution, which was led by Donald A. Matheson, the Caley's engineer-in-chief. Matheson not only increased the concourse to 20 per cent of the area of the platforms but kept it on rising gradients, realigning the platforms so that they terminate before it in echelon, effectively breaking-up large crowds of travellers. Matheson thus outlined his philosophy:

> In planning the probability of crowding and the tendency of people to spread like flowing water and travel along the line of least resistance was kept in view. It was therefore thought desirable to have curved building lines and rounded corners not only in the concourse but also in the subway and elsewhere in the station and this idea was maintained throughout.

The arcade of octagonal steel columns between platforms 9 and 10 marks the boundary of the old station with the new, and were claimed by Matheson (who had used a similar arrange-

41

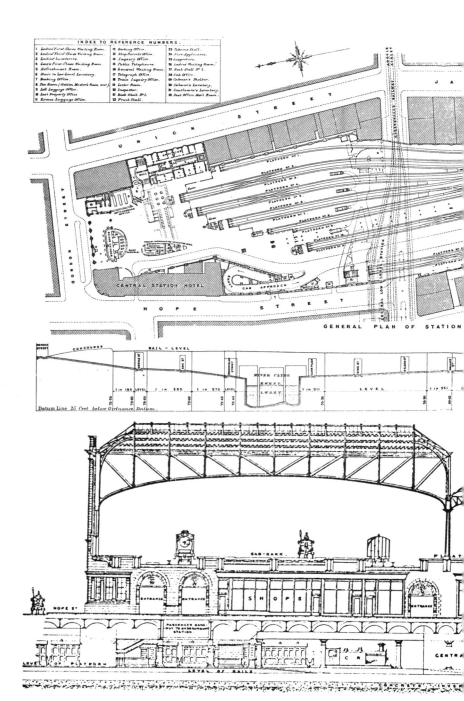

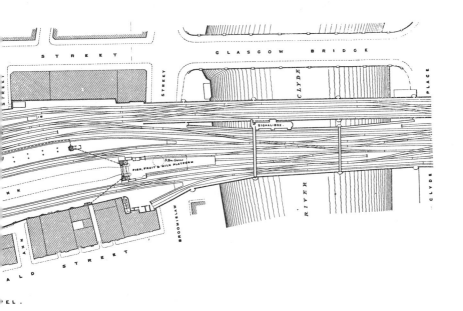

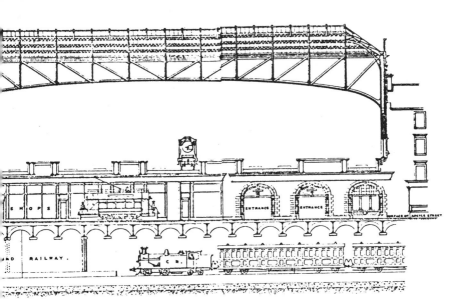

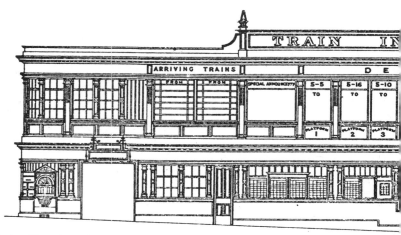

Fig 8  Elevation of destination screen, Central Station, showing its admirable clarity.

ment at Wemyss Bay) 'to form three avenues for traffic—the central avenue for the wheeling of luggage, and an avenue on either side for passengers'. According to James Miller, the Caledonian's architectural consultant, the roof they support 'showed evidence of study in French work'. In fact what Matheson had done was to make the bottom flanges of his girders elliptical 'in order to relieve the depressing effect from their solidity and heaviness' (Fig 9). In 1904 the interior of Bridge Street Station was gutted to make way for much-needed carriage sidings and carriage cleaning plant, but the most remarkable improvement was in signalling. Whereas the old station needed three manually-operated boxes with a staff of 22, the new station had only one box, manned by ten men.

Fig 6  *previous page, above* Plan of Central Station as extended. Note the staggering of the platform ends and the rounding of projections in the concourse, to ease the flow of passengers.

Fig 7  *previous page, below* Sectional elevation of Central Station as extended, showing the relationship between the high and low level stations, and the long bridge over Argyle Street. The latter is still known as the 'Highlanders' Umbrella', from the free shelter it provided for Highland exiles in Glasgow in bygone days.

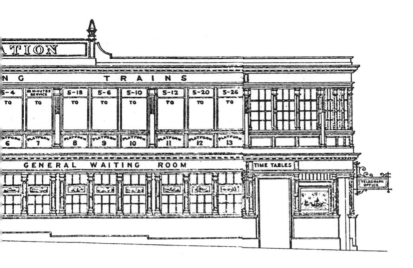

Two storeys high, and 106ft 0in × 16ft 0in (32.3m × 4.9m) it was built on steel supports between the old and new Clyde bridges. By a combination of compressed-air and electro-magnetic equipment, it controlled 137 sets of points. When it came into full operation on 3 May 1908, the new locking frame (which had 374 miniature levers, each of which could be moved by a flick of the finger) was the largest of its kind in the world. The signal galleries carried 23 semaphore arms, but with manual working there would have been 63. This had been achieved by the installation of Annett route indicators at each junction. Electro-pneumatic signalling also got rid of yards of open wires, pulleys and bell cranks which would have prevented an extra line of rails being laid on the new bridge. To cater for longer sleeping-car trains, platforms 1, 2 and 11 were lengthened in the late 1930s. In January 1961 the new station box came into operation. Controlling 90 main-line colour-light signals, eight 'Westlyte' shunting signals, 243 track circuits and 157 electro-pneumatic points on 11 miles of track, it rendered superfluous the 1878 viaduct, which was deteriorating badly.

Fig 9  Perspective sketch of extension, Central Station, showing the spacious cab rank. The platforms on the left were for the mainline arrivals, and those on the right for Gourock and Wemyss Bay trains.

On 11 December 1972 the overhead wires for the 'Electric Scots' crossed the Border. Unlike those south of Crewe they are simpler and cheaper, for they are hung from headspan wires instead of steel portals. The headspan system had already been used on Glasgow suburban routes, whose Cathcart switching station now controls the power to Tebay at the foot of Shap. On paper it sounds like an easy plugging-in operation, until one remembers the amount of preparatory work that had to be done without unduly disrupting passenger services. As with the Clyde Coast and Queen Street projects of the mid-1960s, BR relied on managers co-ordinating with the aid of computers.

Obtaining the necessary headroom for electrification involved some drastic civil engineering. All in all, some 100 bridges between Glasgow and Carlisle were altered or replaced. The 4-track bridge over Cook Street near Central Station was a particularly awkward customer, for its Victorian designers had built part of it into a tenement block, and for four days the Cathcart Circle was closed, Anglo-Scottish trains running via Paisley, Kilmarnock, and Dumfries. In the tunnel beneath Eglinton Street and Pollokshaws Road head-room was achieved by replacing ballast and sleepers with continuous concrete-based track, the first in Britain to be laid on a sharp curve in a tunnel. On 2 November 1970 a £5.1 million contract was signed with BEC–General Signal Ltd, for resignalling the Scottish section of the London line. It was not only the largest single railway contract ever placed in Scotland, but was the death warrant for close on 100 traditional signal cabins. Now, as far as Kirkpatrick in Dumfriesshire (when the Carlisle box takes over) everything is monitored from Glasgow Central and Motherwell through 20 lineside relay rooms. Controlling 277 single track miles of running line making up 123 route miles containing 545 colour-light signals and 329 point machines, Motherwell signalling centre is one of the most advanced in Europe. Its computerised train description system in which trains are identified by 4-digit codes and its push-button controls make it hard to believe that in 1960 we were being moved and guided by a very Victorian technology. Donald Matheson, whose reconstructed Central Station had cost at least £1 million, once remarked that there 'Should be due regard to engineering economies meaning thereby the science of so spending money in the acquirement of land and in the design and construction of works as will tend to ensure adequate financial return on commercial enterprise'. Not counting extras, £55 million was needed to pave the way for the 'Electric Scots' but this spin-off has not been confined just to them. The Hamilton Circle and Lanark line is now all-electric with at least four trains per hour during weekdays and two on Sundays, while since 1973 all stations on the Glasgow–Gourock–Wemyss Bay line have operated yellow tickets on the stored-journey system. Unlike the traditional season tickets, these are transferable and are checked and collected automatically. To quote a recent press notice:

the ticket is inserted into a slot in the barrier equipment, the ticket is 'read' and if valid the turnstile for entry is released and the ticket released to the passenger. At the same time the number of journeys remaining are shown on an indicator on top of the barrier so that every passenger knows exactly how many more times they may use that particular ticket.

We have used this system at platform 12 in Central Station and found it wonderfully efficient but suspect that the 'call for aid' button is not just for regulars who get stuck in the barriers but for those countless Edinburghians who have never had their tickets electronically clipped. On the debit side, we must mention that like Queen Street, policing the approach lines is a non-stop job. During the main line electrification, at least 100 individuals were charged with helping themselves to copper and brass. Now that everything is live such exploits are not so easy but teenage vandalism is still prevalent. As far as passengers are concerned, one of the worst incidents occurred at Motherwell on 12 June 1974. Four suburban trains were trapped in a section and had to be rescued by diesel, two-hour delays were experienced on the Hamilton Circle, and inter-city trains were 39 minutes late.

The most lasting impression the traveller and enthusiast has of Central is its size, noise and complexity. Whereas in half an hour Queen Street has revealed its secrets, at Central there is no point from which to survey the whole scene. B. H. Blyth called Matheson's concourse 'the sheltering place of the public in bad weather, they went there in hundreds, having no intention whatever either of travelling by train themselves or of meeting friends by train'. What he ignored was its uncanny ability to direct and scatter, to let you explore, but not explore everything at one go. The concourse is a substitute for George Square. Though the grass is lacking, the oval Edwardian plaque near platform 10 proclaims that this is the brave new world of 'Speedwell Asphalte'. Whether it is a hell or a paradise we are not quite clear, but the lack of benches (in the end BR did concede a few near platform 13) may deter you from staying too long. Despite the current economic uncertainties the powers-that-be are determined to keep Central at the top of the railway league. From May 1975 the number of trains per day to Kilmarnock and Barrhead was increased from 16 to 21 and by 1977 a £2 million carriage cleaning and maintenance depot for the Glasgow–Euston services was fully operational at Polmadie. In 1979 Central Low Level will reopen to serve the two spurs being built to link the north and south bank electric schemes.

# 3

# ST ENOCH STATION

When the Merchant's Steeple (seventeenth century) was to your left and Milne's Old Wynd Ice Factory (steam century) was to your right, your destination was St Enoch. St Enoch (the name derives from a Glasgow church, not a renegade politician) was Glasgow's answer to London's St Pancras. The accent was on gothic functionalism, and although there was little stained glass on show, steam and smoke were quickly found to be cheap and lively substitutes for choirs and incense. On the concourse, the clock could have stopped at 1901, but for Sir Robert Lorimer's anti-gothic memorial to those employees of the Glasgow & South Western Railway who had fallen in World War I. St Enoch symbolised another war—the Glasgow 'battle of the companies', a GSW 'victory' over the Caledonian. In 1880 it was Scotland's premier passenger terminal, with an hotel to match. In 1950 it might be on crutches, but one thing it never lacked was mystery. The complex was remarkable for the number of entrances. Off the passage parallel to Dunlop Street was a grimy underground booking office with stairs leading to all the platforms. From Maxwell Street a stairway got you right onto the concourse. In St Enoch Square a cluster of rather tatty shops and refreshment bars huddled beneath gothic arches supporting a 1 in 13 terraced carriageway, with a central iron-and-glass gothic verandah having four doorways to the main booking hall. At the top of the terrace, vehicles used a muscular cast-iron portal. Hotel patrons (if they wished to avoid the trains or being classed as tradesmen) used a fussy little groined open porch at the foot of the gothic parade within shouting distance of those office requisites which were a 'boon and a blessing to men' (Introduction).

*Plates 5 and 6. (Above)* Bridge Street Station as rebuilt, *circa* 1885, with Caledonian Railway 2–4–0 No 105. The resemblance to the first part of Central Station is notable. The through roads from Central are on the right. *(Below)* Bridge Street Station and the first Clyde Viaduct, on 2 August 1901, with preparations beginning for the construction of the new viaduct. In the foreground is the old Broomielaw steamboat quay. [*T. R. Annan & Son; Sir William Arrol & Co Ltd*]

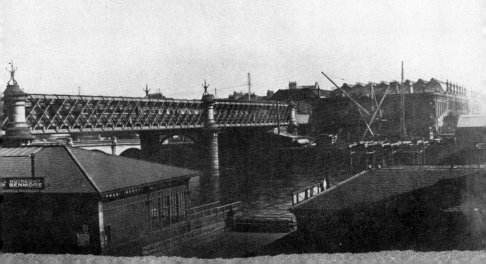

*Plate* 7. The undercroft of the first Central Station under construction in 1877. Note the extensive use of derrick cranes, a Glasgow invention. [*Blyth & Blyth*]

St Enoch was by far the gloomiest of the Glasgow terminal quartet. The train indicator looked like a rood screen in a church, while the monkish booking office within praying distance of the carriageway gave the impression that it was designed for larger traffic which might come on the excommunication of the motor car. The hydraulic hoists on the platforms were entombed in little corbelled wooden boxes which to the uninitiated might have been confessionals. On the concourse a squalid rail bar served as a refectory. For angels, there were pigeons and starlings who, ignoring the blast of engines and wire netting hung up beneath the edge of the roof, unsanctimoniously deposited their offerings on both believers and heretics. Communion (or rather the devil) was represented by the spirituous aroma of whisky from bonded warehouses under the station. The main departure platforms were numbers 1 and 2. Number 1 was the longest and continued to the edge of the bridge over Stockwell Street, where there was a water tower used extensively by station pilots. Because of the sharp curve on the bridge, trains entering and leaving produced an intense squealing noise which was particularly pronounced in the case of large-wheeled locomotives like the LMS Class 2P 4–4–0. It was an experience to be backed out of St Enoch round the triangle at Saltmarket and Clyde Junctions. In the middle of this geometrical necessity (even in 1883 land was at a premium) you could see up to five locomotives waiting in sidings beside a rather worn-out shed. Here, too, sat the signal box installed by the LMS in 1933 in anticipation of a German invasion, or so it seemed, for it appeared to be constructed from thick armour plate.

Apart from locals to Carlisle, Renfrew, East Kilbride, Ayr, Ardrossan, Fairlie and Largs, in the early 1950s there were one or two London trains a day, the principal being the Thames–Clyde Express. At this period, the sort of locomotives which frequented St Enoch (the colloquial Glasgow name is 'St Enoch's') were LMS Class 2P and compound 4–4–0s, Fairburn 2–6–4 tanks, rebuilt Royal Scots, Jubilees, and Black

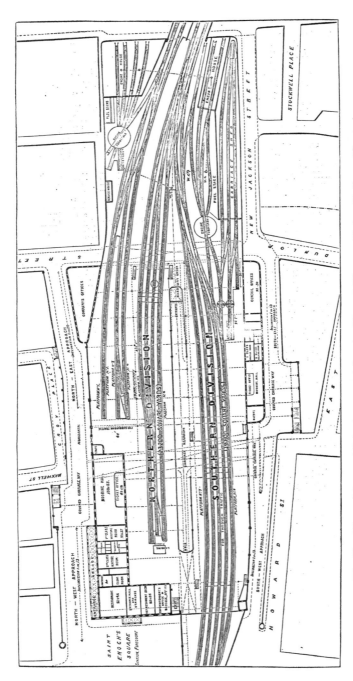

Fig 10  Plan of first published proposal for the City of Glasgow Union Railway 'Central Station', 1867. Note the 'engine houses' on the right.

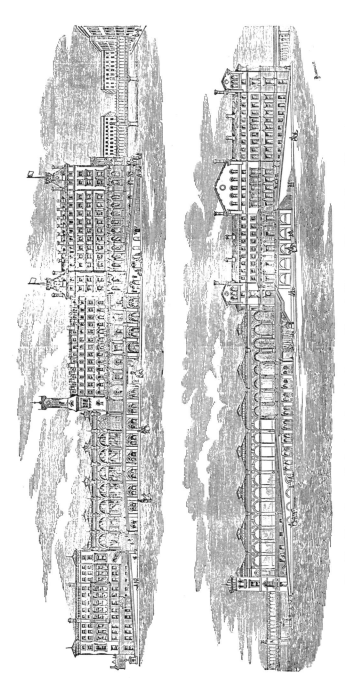

Fig 11   Elevations of north and south fronts, City of Glasgow Union Railway 'Central Station', 1867. The north front (*above*) shows the offices (*left*) and hotel (*right*), with the through lines to the west on the far right. The south front (*below*) has more offices on the right.

Fives. The station pilots were Caledonian Railway 0–4–4 tanks. Of BR standard types, the most common were Class 4MT 2–6–4 tanks, 2–6–0s, Class 5MT 4–6–0s and Clan Pacifics. Unusual visitors were Peppercorn A1 Pacifics which ran for a time on the west coast routes. Class A3 Pacifics were later used on the Thames–Clyde Express. Before closure, diesel traction had been introduced on the Midland route with Class 45s and 46s, and Swindon-built Inter-City multiple-unit railcars on the Ayr line. For the use of the civil engineers who occupied a labyrinth of offices beyond the St Enoch Hotel, an inspection saloon was almost invariably parked on the siding between platforms 1 and 2.

### The Making of St Enoch

The G&SW faced similar problems to the Caledonian in penetrating the city centre. Land values were high, proprietors tediously numerous and there was inevitably the unpopular river crossing. Fortunately the opposition to a bridge at Hutchesontown was less than the Caley encountered further down river at the Broomielaw. The agency for the construction of the new terminus and its connecting lines was the City of Glasgow Union Railway, promoted by the Edinburgh & Glasgow and G&SW in 1864. The initial authorised capital was £900,000, but in 1865 when the E&G merged with the North British Railway it was increased by £140,000, a reflection of rising prices in a boom. The main line of the CGU started on the Glasgow & Paisley Joint line at Pollok Junction, swung eastward to Gorbals Junction, then crossed the Clyde on a two-track bridge, finally turning east and north to join the Sighthill branch of the NB at Springburn. A branch ran from Port Eglinton Junction west and north to join the line leading to General Terminus, and the NB extended its Coatbridge branch to the site of the old University in High Street (see Chapter 6).

The original 'St Enoch's Square Central Station' was, as planned by John Fowler and J. F. Blair (Figs 10, 11), a through station with eight platforms, two locomotive sheds and a carriage shed (*Engineering*, 18 January 1867). To save space, sector plates were to be used instead of conventional points at the ends of two of the platforms. A 'grand hotel' formed part of the North frontage. The proposed station was to have occupied almost exactly the site of that actually built, though the through lines to the west were never constructed. The roof was intended to be in three spans, 105ft 0in, 95ft 0in, and 85ft 0in (32.0m, 30.0m, and 27.0m) wide. The main station was designed in Italianate style, with a French hotel block. When the Union Bill was promoted it was vaguely suggested that the new terminal could be used by other companies, but this was probably a gambit. On 15 November 1867 representatives of the G&SW and Caledonian met at the Queen's Hotel in Glasgow. Speaking for the G&SW, Sir Andrew Orr said that just to obtain the right of access to the new station (but not the use) would require at least £300,000, but if the Caledonian wished, it could later apply 'and come in upon terms to be arranged'. The G&SW was probably influenced by the Midland Railway in pursuing this policy. A Bill for the amalgamation of these two companies had been put forward earlier in the year, though it was thrown out. In the following year the directors of the Midland explicitly warned the G&SW to allow nothing to the Caledonian.

In August 1868 the South Western board reported that £300,000 had already been spent 'on works as yet entirely unproductive'. Construction had not yet begun on the terminal in St Enoch Square, where compensation to property owners was now approaching £200,000. The area was a tricky one, filled with warehouses, printing offices, a tube works and a music hall. When the CGU solicitors drew up a map, they found at least 154 distinct plots of ground where ownership was by no means clear. It was imperative to the G&SW that a temporary station be built on the north bank. Bridge Street was already overcrowded and could not accommodate the traffic expected when the Greenock line was opened. The decision was therefore made to erect a temporary station at Dunlop Street at an estimated cost of £200,000. The directors then agreed to guarantee the interest on so much of the preference stock of the CGU as would be necessary to meet the cost, though this required the approval of Parliament as well as of the shareholders. Fortunately, an Act of 1867 had already given authority to increase the capital by £140,000, thus reducing by £7,000 the rent the G&SW would have to pay the CGU for the use of the temporary station.

On 2 June 1870 the Earl of Dalkeith ceremonially opened the viaduct over the River Clyde at Hutchesontown. Its wrought-iron lattice girders rested on masonry piers and cast-iron cylinders sunk nearly 80ft 0in (24.4m) into the river bed. Over the water the track was carried on five spans each of 75ft 0in (22.9m); over the streets on each side there was one span of just over 63ft 0in (19.2m). Dunlop Street Station opened on 12 December 1870. Built by Thomas Brassey & Co, it had six lines, four platforms, a booking hall and refreshment room. When it closed with the opening of St Enoch in 1876, it was decided that its roof should be taken down and re-erected when required at the G&SW terminus at Fairlie.

There were further unsuccessful attempts to amalgamate the G&SW and the Midland in 1872 and 1873, while the Settle & Carlisle line, the link between the two companies' systems, was slowly built. Despite the absence of administrative amalgamation, Midland influence on the G&SW was strong, and the Midland's other Scottish partner, the NB, backed-up when required. When in July 1872 the Caledonian re-opened negotiations on the use of the St Enoch terminal, this time with the CGU, the latter replied that it would have to consult the NB, which declined to co-operate. The Caley had then no option but to build a terminal of its own (see Chapter 2), though its usefulness was limited by G&SW intransigence; in June 1874 the South West resolved on no account to sell its interest in Bridge Street Station (see Chapters 1 and 2).

With the completion of the Settle & Carlisle line

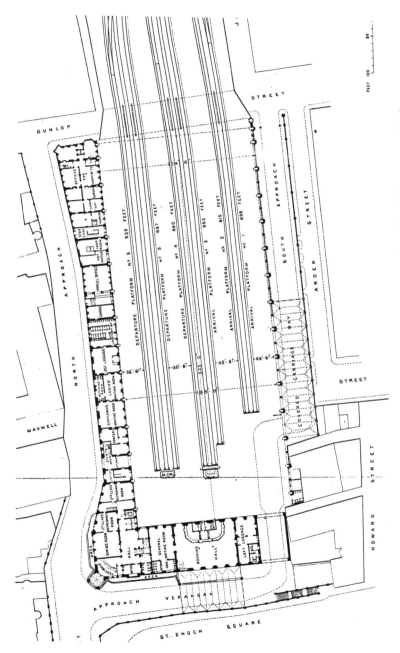

Fig 12   Plan of St Enoch Station as built. The hotel was above the booking hall range on the left.

59

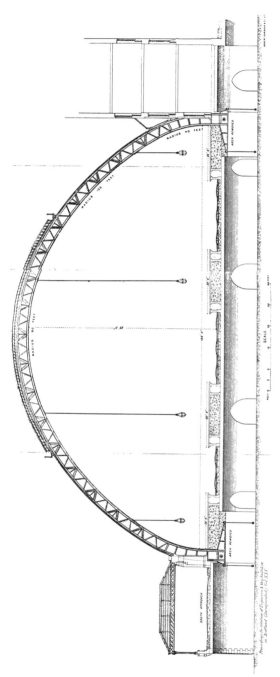

Fig 13 Section of the roof of St Enoch Station as built, showing the absence of any positive connection between the lower ends of the arch ribs.

approaching, the Midland began to take a close interest in the construction of the St Enoch terminal, which would be the station for joint London–Glasgow services. In February 1874 James Allport, the Midland manager, examined alternative plans for the new station, choosing 'the plan with the cab road outside the station'. Midland influence was immediately apparent in the choice of gothic as the style for the station buildings, as at St Pancras, and by the allocation of the contract for the St Pancras-style roof to Handyside & Co, a Derby firm.

It was not until August 1874 that most of the properties had been acquired for the extension of the line to St Enoch Square, and by October 1875 Brassey's men had completed the platforms. On 17 October 1876 St Enoch was officially opened by the Prince and Princess of Wales who arrived in a special train consisting of two Pullman cars named *Albion* and *India*. At that time the range of station offices on the north side and the hotel had not been built. As late as 18 July 1876 the Caledonian tried to buy its way into St Enoch, but rapidly broke off talks when the G&SW said that nothing less than £500,000 would do. Quickly the station buildings took shape, but as can be seen from the plan (Fig 12) they were limited by the nature of the site.

A remarkable feature of the station was the train shed roof. It was similar to that at St Pancras, but it terminated in a curved soffit (Fig 13), not a pointed apex, and as shown in the table below, was considerably smaller.

**Table 1: Comparative dimensions of St Pancras and St Enoch station roofs**

|        | St Pancras          | St Enoch            |
|--------|---------------------|---------------------|
| Width  | 243ft in (74.1m)    | 204ft 0in (62.2m)   |
| Height | 110ft 0in (33.5m)   | 83ft 0in (25.3m)    |
| Length | 689ft 0in (210.0m)  | 525ft 0in (160.0m)  |

The ribs consisted of 15 lattice girders each of which was 5ft 0in (1.5m) deep and weighed 36ton 12 cwt (37.2 tonnes). They were just over 36ft 0in (11.0m) apart except at the east end where they were 18ft 0in (5.5m) apart and carried an ornamental screen of glass and iron. The western screen was 35ft 0in (10.7m) above the platforms and ended in a lean-to roof against the wall of the booking office. The directors had originally planned to have a clock with a 7ft 0in (2.1m) dial above the booking office, but thought that a 10ft 0in (3.0m) one costing £330 would be better. In the end, one of 12ft 0in (3.6m) was ordered from John Walker of Cornhill, London for £440 (Plate 15). The floor girders of the train shed did not act as a tie for the roof principals, as they did at St Pancras. Instead, each rib stood on wrought iron shoes secured by bolts 2¼in (57mm) diameter attached to cast-iron anchor beams embedded in the platform walls. Each main rib was delivered from Derby in eleven sections. Using sheer legs the first two were hoisted into position and temporarily supported by timber staging while 3-ton steam cranes running on rails raised the remaining nine. Throughout the work John Fowler was consulting engineer, but following the death of his assistant James F. Blair in August 1876 he was joined by Mr Crouch, whose business associate Charles P. Hogg had been resident engineer from the start. During construction truss rods had to be inserted to correct a lateral deflection on the lower purlins and this is probably why W. H. Barlow (the engineer who designed the St Pancras roof) claimed £315 in professional fees from the G&SW in May 1875. Hogg later admitted that were he to design another similar roof he would be inclined 'to put a little more weight in the purlins and a little less in the arch'. His colleagues seemed satisfied with the end product, but when questioned as to cost, Hogg could give no clear figure, but thought it would be 'about £40 per square of 100 feet (30.5m)'. Crouch's estimate for the whole in December 1876 was £52,000.

As originally built, there were eight lines of rails. Since two of these were used for storing carriages, there were six available platforms. Platforms 1–3 were allocated to arrivals, and platforms 4–6 for departures, but in practice the system was more flexible. A notable innovation was to be found in the train shed. It was the first public area in Glasgow to be regularly lit by electricity. In September 1879 the British Electric Light Company was given the contract for a 12-month experimental period on the understanding that it would cost 4s 5d (22p) per hour, the same sum it cost for illuminating with gas. There were originally four lamps but two more had to be added. Each was of 6000 candlepower and was individually fed by a Gramme machine of the 'A' type. The 15-horsepower needed for the whole installation was provided by a steam engine in the hotel laundry. Serrin lamps were first tried, but were soon replaced by those of Crompton. They were suspended 35ft 0in (10.7m) above the platforms, and could be lowered when necessary to replace the carbons, which had an average life of eight hours. Following discussions with Sir William Thomson, conical reflectors and octagonal glass globes were fitted to improve efficiency. Even so, the original 464 gas jets (which took 30 minutes to light) were kept for emergencies. In October 1882 two more arcs were installed, and two years later a Putman engine (costing £480) was ordered.

As shown in Table 2 St Enoch was an immediate success.

**Table 2: Operating statistics for St Enoch station, 1880–1922**

| Year | Total passengers booked | Total passenger receipts | Total parcel receipts | Total expenses |
|---|---|---|---|---|
| 1880 | 1,420,826 | £131,195 | £ 14,789 | £ 6,645 |
| 1890 | 2,128,498 | 155,898 | 48,736 | 9,492 |
| 1900 | 3,247,767 | 190,093 | 71,550 | 18,860 |
| 1910 | 2,916,124 | 233,019 | 91,120 | 23,320 |
| 1920 | 4,145,900 | 571,379 | 104,665 | 76,074 |
| 1922 | 3,330,869 | 492,260 | 154,673 | 99,563 |

The most important trains were those providing connections with the Midland Railway at Carlisle; by 1902, seven of these were run in each direction daily. With good reason St Enoch was called 'the happy hunting ground of the golfer' as in addition to club courses at Troon, Irvine and Ayr, served by the line, on 17 May 1906 the company opened a station, luxurious hotel, and golfing links at Turnberry. There was also a coast service to Greenock where steamers plied to Dunoon, Rothesay, the Kyles of Bute, Loch Long and the Holy Loch. Ardrossan was an important starting point for Arran and the Isle of Man. In the autumn of 1891 fear of Caledonian competition forced the G&SW to buy a fleet of its own; by 1894 gross tonnage had increased from 1250 to 3000 tons. Eventually the wasteful duplication of services was ended by agreement. St Enoch not only handled a heavy fish traffic from Ayrshire ports, but dairy produce from Ayrshire and Dumfriesshire; in the early 1900s nearly 400,000 milk churns passed through the parcels department each year. Express trains ran to Johnstone, Beith, Kilbirnie, Kilwinning, Irvine, Troon, Prestwick, Ayr, Dalmellington, Maybole, Girvan and Stranraer, the last providing a connection with the Irish steamers.

The success of the new station created its own problems, especially in train working. In the early 1880s an average of 140 trains used St Enoch each day. One traveller observing the working of the Glasgow & Paisley Joint line found that many trains travelled in batches at the beginning and end of each hour only, and claimed that this was achieved 'by sending off two trains at the same instant from Central and St Enoch and leaving them to take their chance of getting to Paisley without collision'. In fact the G&SW continued to have a good record for safety. Its worst accident (15 were killed) happened at the end of the Glasgow Fair holidays on 27 July 1903 when a train from Ardrossan entered St Enoch at an excessive speed and collided with the buffer stops.

In the 1880s there was a Tyers train describer to help signalmen set their points and signals, but much delay was caused by goods trains using the College branch, and much shunting was done verbally and by hand signalling. On 3 July 1898 forty-five electric shunting signals based on W. R. Sykes's lock-and-block system came into operation. At least 135 combinations of these signals was possible, and an idea of their

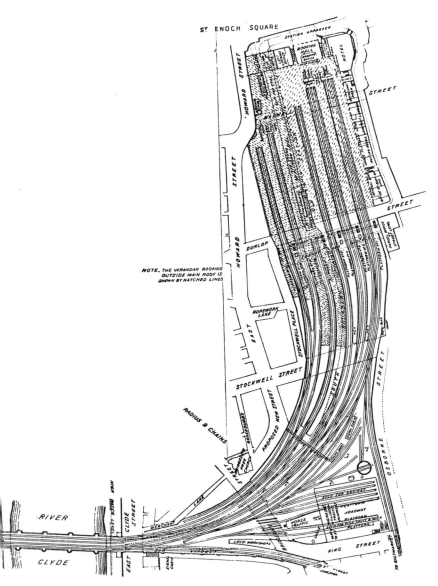

Fig 14   Plan of St Enoch Station as extended, showing also the sharp radius of the approach curve, and the engine shed.

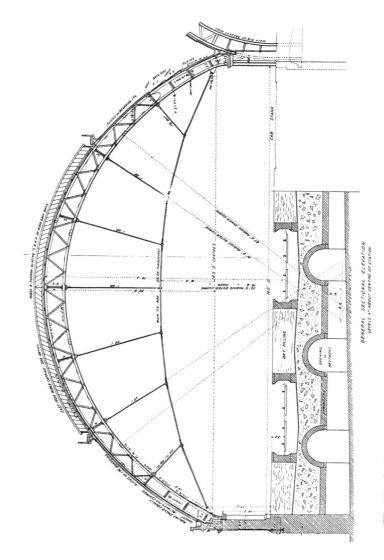

Fig 15   Section of the roof of the extended portion of St Enoch Station, showing the more conventional tied ribs.

significance is given by the fact that around St Enoch the number of levers in cabins was reduced from 393 to 183.

There were, however, obvious limits to what could be achieved by resignalling, and in 1898 powers were obtained for extending the station (Figs 14, 15). Clyde Bridge was reconstructed to give four running lines, and from St Enoch to Port Eglinton Junction the lines were also quadrupled. At the southern end of the station six additional platforms were built, the twelve platforms (all of which were renumbered) covering a total area of 23,600sq yd (19,732m²). Part of the roof was extended by 281ft 0in (85.6m). The new section was of similar design to the old, but was only 65ft 0in (19.8m) high. Near No 1 platform a barbers' shop was installed. In 1904 a writer in *The Railway Magazine* found this establishment comprising 'two handsomely fitted up rooms in which palms and ferns make a very attractive show against the white glazed tiles. In these two rooms no less than eleven unshorn and unkempt passengers can be operated on at once there being a staff of thirteen in all. The dozen or so circular brushes which go to make the department complete are revolved by an electric motor.' The extension cost about £2.3 million, the rates for the whole station in 1904 being £18,070. Station staff of all kinds had increased in number from 20 in 1876 to 220.

An interesting feature of collaboration between the NB and the G&SW was through working between the two systems. Following the extension of the NB line to College on 1 September 1872, through connections were provided to Edinburgh and Ayrshire via Coatbridge and Bellgrove in the following manner. Part of the NB train from Coatbridge, being uncoupled at Bellgrove, was moved to Clyde Junction to join the train from St Enoch. In the opposite direction coaches were detached from the G&SW train at Shields Road where a NB locomotive took it to Bellgrove to join an express to Edinburgh via Bathgate. From 1 July 1885 this system became more flexible, for if the Ayrshire coast train left from either platform 5 or 6, the Saltmarket Spur could be used to connect it with the coaches from Coatbridge, and there was no need to use Clyde Junction. However, by developing its Dunbarton-shire lines, the Caledonian after 1896 could bring passengers from Airdrie and Coatbridge into Central Low Level where they could change without difficulty to High Level for trains to Ayrshire.

To meet this competition, on 27 October 1897 representa-tives of the G&SW and NB met at the Railway Clearing House in London to consider improvements in Ayrshire and Edin-burgh connections. Unfortunately, the NB had to admit that more frequent services using the existing system were really out of the question. Additional main line trains stopping at Cowlairs West Junction would be inconvenient, and if connec-tions were made at Cowlairs Station there would be much shunting and delay. (Cowlairs Incline had enough already!) In addition there was already a heavy goods traffic over the line between Cowlairs West Junction, Sighthill, Bellgrove, Park-head and College, which would be delayed by passenger trains, bookings on which had already been badly affected by Cale-donian competition. Hence on 4 December 1897 the NB suggested an omnibus service as an alternative for 'the expense would certainly be very much less than the expense in working the through connections via Springburn'.

On 1 May 1899 the two companies started running omni-buses between St Enoch and Queen Street. From 8.00am to 7.40pm there was a 20-minute service. Passengers with through tickets travelled free, others 'when there is room' at one penny ($\frac{1}{2}$p) per single journey. It was suggested that an 'electric bus' be tried, but this never got beyond the design stage. Trouble soon developed between NB and G&SW man-agements; two omnibus companies were employed, but be-cause of an agreement with the G&SW, one firm refused to collect any fares! Worse than this, the lessee for cabs at Queen Street, who charged one shilling (5p) for his services, felt his in-terests threatened. The G&SW broke off negotiations and in 1902 both buses and through trains vanished.

*Plates 8 and 9. (Above)* Excavating the foundations for the first Clyde Viaduct, in 1876. Note the elaborate gantry crane worked from the stationary steam engine in the centre, and the portable steam engine on the right. (*Below*) The Central Station Hotel under construction in 1880. Note that the corner has been demolished during the conversion from offices to hotel. [*Both, Blyth & Blyth*]

Plates 10 and 11. (*Above*) The Central Station Hotel as completed in 1886. (*Below*) The interior of the first Central Station, showing the cramped circulating area. The platforms are numbered in the reverse order to the present sequence. [*Illustrated London News; Pennycook Patent Glazing Co Ltd*]

Though as at Central main line services continued to develop, after 1900 the few G&SW inner suburban routes, as on the Caley, could not withstand competition from the electric tram. On 30 September 1902 regular passenger traffic ceased between Govan and Springburn. Garngad Station closed on 1 March 1910, Gallowgate Central in 1917, and from 1 January of that last year no more suburban trains left St Enoch for Paisley.

## The St Enoch Hotel

Writing in the *Glasgow News* on 18 February 1881, a correspondent remarked that before the growth of railways in Glasgow there were three main types of hotels—'the Royal', 'the William' and 'McWhiskeys'. The first was filthy and expensive, the second filthier and cheap, and in the last 'the redoubtable McWhiskey was so convinced of the superiority of his own liquids as frequently to present himself before his guests in a condition of noisy and offensive conviviality'. The St Enoch Hotel (Plate 14) was not the city's first station hotel, but with over 200 bedrooms and 20 public rooms it was the biggest and when it opened on 3 July 1879, the largest in Scotland. The main frontage to St Enoch Square was 360ft 0in (110m) long and 120ft 0in (36.6m) high. The north wing extended from St Enoch Square to Dunlop Street for just over 500ft 0in (153m). The building lacked a tower, but this was compensated for by an impressive grouping of pointed dormers and heavy chimney stacks. It was no doubt Midland influence which gave Mr Thomas Willson of Hampstead the commission for this massive building, but he was assisted by Miles S. Gibson, a Glasgow architect with by no means insignificant ecclesiastical experience. Much was also contributed by James F. Blair, consulting engineer to the CGU.

James Watson & Sons of Glasgow started construction in 1876, though it was not until February 1877 that the South Western firmly committed itself to retaining control of the hotel. In February 1878 a committee went to London to consult with Mr R Etzensberger as to hotel furnishings at St Enoch. Etzensberger was St Pancras's first manager, but financial considerations made the interior of St Enoch a visual disappointment when compared with its London equivalent. Rooms on the first floor were the most lavishly fitted, being furnished throughout by Gillow & Co. Only the first three floors were of fire-resistant construction, but those in the remaining three could comfort themselves by knowing that on the roof were tanks holding five thousand gallons of water for use in the event of fire. The staff of 80 had dormitories on the sixth floor. Here the corridors were 10ft 0in (3.0m) wide, 2ft 0in (0.6m) less than at St Pancras.

Full use was made of the latest devices of the age. The kitchen, measuring 85ft 0in × 32ft 0in (25.9m × 9.8m), was equipped by Jeakes and Company of London, the contractors who fitted-up the St Pancras kitchens. There were four of Messrs A. & P. Stevens' self-acting food hoists, and an ice safe 'capable of storing 25 tons [25.3 tonnes] of ice'. For passengers and luggage the building had two 'self acting ascending rooms', worked by high-pressure water piped from an accumulator used for working the hydraulic cranes at College Goods Station. The hotel also boasted an extensive system of electric bells installed by John Bryden & Sons of Birmingham. The busy Victorian executive was not forgotten for 'on each floor there is a letter box which communicates with a large box in the hall below. The box in the hall is cleared for every mail, so that a letter dropped into the box, say on the fifth floor, will reach its destination with the same punctuality as if it had been placed in the first instance in the General Post Office'.

On 30 April 1878 the G&SW appointed as the hotel's first manager E. W. Theim, a man of 'not only metropolitan but cosmopolitan experience'. For a time the company had a virtual monopoly of modern hotel accommodation in the city (Fig 16) and the *Ayr Advertiser* correctly summarised this state of affairs when it said that 'the locality of the railway station is

## ST. ENOCH STATION HOTEL, GLASGOW.

E. W. THIEM, Manager.

### TARIFF OF CHARGES FOR APARTMENTS
*(INCLUDING ATTENDANCE).*

#### FIRST FLOOR.
| | £ | s. | d. |
|---|---|---|---|
| Parlour and 3 Double Bedrooms, *en suite* | 1 | 11 | 6 |
| Private Sitting-Rooms . . . . . . . . from | 0 | 10 | 6 |
| Double Bedrooms . . . . . . . . . . . | 0 | 7 | 6 |

#### SECOND FLOOR.
| | £ | s. | d. |
|---|---|---|---|
| Sitting-Room and 3 Double Bedrooms, *en suite* | 1 | 5 | 0 |
| Sitting-Rooms . . . . . . . . . . from | 0 | 7 | 6 |
| Double Bedrooms . . . . . . . . from | 0 | 6 | 0 |
| Single Bedrooms . . . . . . . . from | 0 | 4 | 0 |

#### THIRD FLOOR.
| | £ | s. | d. |
|---|---|---|---|
| Sitting-Room and 3 Double Bedrooms, *en suite* | 1 | 1 | 0 |
| Sitting-Rooms . . . . . . . . . . from | 0 | 5 | 0 |
| Double Bedrooms . . . . . . . . from | 0 | 4 | 6 |
| Single Bedrooms . . . . . . . . from | 0 | 3 | 6 |

#### FOURTH FLOOR.
| | £ | s. | d. |
|---|---|---|---|
| Double Bedrooms . . . . . . . . from | 0 | 4 | 0 |
| Single Bedrooms . . . . . . . . from | 0 | 2 | 6 |

#### FIFTH FLOOR.
| | £ | s. | d. |
|---|---|---|---|
| Double Bedrooms . . . . . . . . from | 0 | 3 | 6 |
| Single Bedrooms . . . . . . . . from | 0 | 2 | 6 |
| Visitors' Servants' Rooms . . . . . . . . | 0 | 1 | 6 |

Where Bedrooms are occupied by two persons an extra charge of 1s. is made.

The Charges for Bedrooms vary according to position.

| | £ | s. | d. |
|---|---|---|---|
| Fires in Parlours . . . . . . . . per Day | 0 | 2 | 0 |
| Fires in Bedrooms. . . . . . . per Night | 0 | 1 | 0 |
| Lights in Parlours . . . . . . . . ,, ,, | 0 | 1 | 6 |
| Baths in Bathroom (Hot or Cold). . . . . . | 0 | 1 | 0 |
| Baths (Sponge or Sitz) . . . . . . . . | 0 | 0 | 6 |

### TARIFF OF CHARGES IN COFFEE-ROOM.

| | s. | d. |
|---|---|---|
| Breakfast (Table d'Hôte) . . . . . . . . . . . | 2 | 6 |
| Luncheons (Cold Meat, Vegetables, and Cheese) . . . | 2 | 0 |
| Dinner (Table d'Hôte), at 4 P.M. . . . . . . . . | 3 | 6 |
| ,, ,, at 6.30 P.M. . . . . . . . | 4 | 6 |
| Cup of Tea, Coffee, or Chocolate . . . . . . . . | 0 | 6 |
| Tea, Coffee, or Chocolate, with Bread and Butter, Toast, or Muffins and Preserves . . . . . . . | 2 | 0 |
| Do., with Eggs or Cold Meat . . . . . . . . . | 2 | 6 |
| Do., with Fried or Broiled Fish . . . . . . . . | 2 | 6 |
| Do., with Hot Meat . . . . . . . . . . . | 3 | 0 |
| Soups, with Bread, per Basin . . . . . . . . . | 1 | 0 |

Dinners, Luncheons, and Suppers, *à la carte*, as per Daily Bill of Fare.

| | s. | d. |
|---|---|---|
| Visitors' Servants' Board per diem . . . . . . . | 5 | 0 |

For Meals served in Apartments an Extra Charge will be made.

———o———

The Charge for Apartments includes *all* Attendance and the entire Service of the Company are *not* entitled to any fees or gratuities whatever from Visitors.

The Accounts are presented Weekly for payment, except in special cases, when they will be presented Daily.

Visitors are requested to give their names on arrival, to prevent delay in the delivery of Letters, &c., addressed to them.

Dogs are not permitted in Apartments.

Smoking permitted in the Smoking and Billiard Rooms only.

Fig 16  Proposed tariff, St Enoch Station Hotel, 1879, as submitted to the G&SW Hotel Committee.

becoming generally the recognised place for a good hotel . . . a tendency of this kind is irresistible as the flow of the tide'. The Caledonian therefore had to have its own plush hotel, and got it, but only at considerable expense (Chapter 2). In 1886 the G&SW opened a new station and hotel at Ayr. Smaller than

St Enoch, it cost £50,000. The buildings, designed by the G&SW engineer Andrew Galloway, were not gothic but seemed to exhibit 'a free treatment of classic after a simple renaissance character'. The company was soon offering weekend accommodation in Ayr and first-class return travel to Glasgow, all for 25 shillings (£1.25) per head. This was for the wealthy minority, but the battle of the hotels was on. The *Glasgow Herald* warned of the 'threatened monopoly of railway caravanseries'; others of 'railway poaching', and the absence in the G&SW printed reports of the profits from its hotels. In 1881 proprietors of Edinburgh hostelries attempted to stir up feeling in the Glasgow press. Donald MacGregor of the Royal Hotel saw station hotels 'at variance with free trade and the functions of a railway', but Edinburgh got its large station hotels in the late 1890s, with comparable effect.

Well built and well designed, St Enoch Station was an example to be imitated by the G&SW's rivals. However, by 1910 it had been out-classed by Central Station and following the rationalisation of the inter- and post-war years it became increasingly obsolete. It is significant that no drastic modernisation, apart from resignalling, took place after 1904, and until closure in 1966 the station retained much of its Victorian flavour. The hotel was closed in 1974 because it failed to comply with new fire regulations. The interior was not exactly as it was in E. W. Theim's day but the wealth of marble fireplaces, varnished woodwork, and the elaborately engraved opaque glass in the bedroom doors gave a strong if not overwhelming Victorian atmosphere. St Enoch was truly gothic, but in this respect it did not set a trend, for by 1880 secular gothic was already falling out of favour with both architects and the public. As *The Builder* put it in 1898 'The great mass of the St Enoch railway station is a Gothic revival effort that one can no longer sympathise with; considered a success in its day, its pointed segmental arches and heavy mock machicolations now seem the acme of ugliness.'

# 4

# QUEEN STREET STATION

Queen Street High Level, originally the western terminus of the Edinburgh & Glasgow Railway, was opened on 18 February 1842. The oldest surviving station within the city boundaries, it serves the second busiest inter-city route in Britain. Edinburgh, that other world, is 47 miles away and since 3 May 1971 can be reached in 43 minutes. On an average weekday no fewer than 60 trains have linked the two capitals of Scotland. Traffic is said to increase at the rate of 7 per cent a year, and yet the line is not even electrified. Before 1971 the journey took 55 minutes and trains had buffet cars. The 'new look' coaches and their push-and-pull diesels have grown shabbier because of over-use and current restrictions on public investment, but this seems to be no deterrent to passengers. At rush-hours the Edinburgh trains at platform 2 are virtually bursting at the seams. Standing on inter-city is an injury, but in the 1840s the E&G had no scruples about insulting its patrons:

> The moment the time arrived for a train to start, a bell was rung, and the doors leading to the booking offices were locked, and simultaneously with their closing . . . a blunt guillotine was lowered. This prevented all access to the departure platform . . . if passengers ran round to the Queen Street entrance there was a chance of catching the train, but at Queen Street their progress was arrested by an elderly official armed with a thick stick.

While Queen Street lacks the imperial vistas of Central Station, it boasts one of the most dramatic of urban railway approaches in Britain. From Cowlairs, your train is on a 2090yd

(1911m) incline entombed in the living rock. Derelict factories and modern multi-storeys loom overhead while old pram bodies and car tyres beside the permanent way betray the presence of the predatory vandal; in the 1960s this line was reputed to receive the greatest number of brickbats in Western Europe. For the final lap, you screech down a half-mile tunnel. A living memorial to that engineering genius, John Miller, it was exhibited to the public early in January 1842, raising the princely sum of £218–19–10d (£218.99) for navvies injured during its construction. The narrow concourse, the funereal tunnel portal, and an adjacent parcels depot (which smelt of West Highland fish traffic) gave High Level in the steam era a coughing, noisy and claustrophobic atmosphere. The demise of steam in 1965 gave the green light for modernisation. The buffer stops were put in line and a £300,000 telecommunications centre serving the whole of the Glasgow network installed. The new system of colour-light signalling is worked from Cowlairs and comprises 13 colour-light and 13 subsidiary signals. The goods station was demolished to make way for a car park, taxi ranks, telephones, a superloo, and a gleaming row of left luggage lockers. This area is in effect a second concourse and is easily reached by a wide passage at the take-away kiosk near platform 7. The new travel centre and staff offices at the west end of the old concourse were opened on 19 May 1969 at a cost of £200,000 plus a pair of shoes and trousers. Ignoring all warnings, a youth had rushed through a barrier and promptly sank up to his knees in quick-setting concrete. Before workmen could do anything, he struggled out and 'ran to catch his train, still covered in concrete, which was hardening every second'.

The small plastic seating unit with the potted plant in the middle is an attractive if somewhat incongruous addition to the new-look concourse, for after a train arrives, in no time at all the crowd moves off to the flowers and benches in George Square or the gloom of Queen Street Low Level Station. Many are also sucked into 'the largest single complex so far built in

BR catering's development plans in Scotland or England'. Costing £280,000 The George cafeteria, the Hebridean restaurant and the Highlander and Clyde bars have officially been in business since 27 March 1973; after a quick one in the noisy Clyde, you drift down to a table in the urbane Hebridean. The Oregon pine ceiling, the blue-green patterned carpet, the tartan-skirted waitresses and Robert Stewart's impressionistic mural of the Hebrides (the theme of which is continued in the menu cards and place mats) remind one that the 'Second City' will never be an English one.

Metropolitan sophistication never quite reached the adjacent North British Hotel. Pre-dating the railway, it is one of the original buildings in George Square and in E&G days was known as the Queen's Hotel. In 1933 there were 84 bedrooms each with a coal fire but no H&C. Completely refurbished and extended in the early 1970s, the 'NB' is now the fourth largest railway hotel in Scotland, but it owes its success to location more than anything else. Its mutilated classical façade demanded drastic treatment in the form of cement and paint. The end result, far from being a disaster, is positively inviting.

Table 3:   Queen Street High Level platforms

| Platform | Length in feet |
|---|---|
| 1 | 460 |
| 2 | 590 |
| 3 | 460 |
| 4 | 460 |
| 5 | 590 |
| 6 | 590 |
| 7 | 660 |

Platform 1 (the only one not under the great roof) is in the darkest corner of the station and is used by Falkirk (Grahamston) trains. Platforms 3–7 serve the Dundee, Perth, Stirling, Aberdeen, Inverness and West Highland lines. For the benefit of Edinburgh folk, some of the columns at platform 2 have been smartened up with mosaic and concrete. Comparison with Central Station traffic figures is interesting.

**Table 4:** **Passenger comparisons Queen Street/Central Stations**

*Average weekday (November 1974)*

|  | Passengers | Trains |
|---|---|---|
| Central | 82598 | 963 |
| Queen Street (High Level) | 19499 | 163 |
| Queen Street (Low Level) | 43858 | 300 |

Low Level (officially known since 1960 as Queen Street Electric Station) is a grimly functional cavern serving the north bank suburban lines of the old Glasgow & District Railway. Since remodelling in 1959–60 westbound trains (to Helensburgh, Balloch, Milngavie, Hyndland, etc) have used platform 10, which is totally separated by a wall from the eastbound trains at platform 11. This wall is said to have the 'effect of reducing noise and giving the maximum simplicity and cleanliness of structure' and is used for advertising and system route diagrams, but to the enthusiast it is a visual vexation. The mathematically-minded, too, soon feel ill at ease. What has happened is that the reconstructed Low Level lost platforms 8 and 9, but as a mark of respect to the age of steam, these numbers could never be used again!

The blue electrics of the north bank have a character all their own. They will take you to the old shipyards, old tenements at Clydebank, the Cameron wildlife park on the shores of Loch Lomond, or the stockbroker belt at Bearsden. Inaugurated by Sir Brian Robertson on 5 November 1960 these Blue Trains were a dress rehearsal for the later electrification projects, but Sir Brian's remark that the system 'will probably take a little bit of time to get run in' was prophetic. Following a series of transformer explosions (one at Renton injured two passengers) steam was re-introduced on Monday 19 December, locomotives being brought from as far away as Edinburgh, Ardrossan, and Hawick. The Blue Trains returned on 10 October 1961. Of the 329 which ran during the following day 310 were on time while of the remaining 19 only two were more than five minutes late. Within a month, passenger receipts had increased by 142 per cent. The Blue Trains (though a few purists might object to Caledonian blue on an NB route) became the image of modernity, and in Glasgow are the best legacy of the 'swinging sixties'. In 1966 north side station staff became the first in Scotland to wear the new continental-style uniforms.

## The 'Boat' Trains

Between 17.00 and 21.00 on 28 September 1976 some 14 million tons of rain fell on Glasgow, the greatest deluge since 1884. In no time at all lift shafts flooded, and road and rail traffic ground to a halt. Worst hit was Queen Street Station. From century-old sewers a cascade of water rushed down the tunnel putting all seven platforms out of action. Only with difficulty did the 18.30 'sail' for Edinburgh. The water quickly found its own level by pouring through to Low Level, demolishing in the process part of a tiled wall and ceiling canopy of the westbound platform. The station approaches were not much better. Trains from Oban and Fort William were stranded at Dumbarton, and the 14.05 ex-Mallaig could not get beyond Possil. At Springburn Station, passengers on the 17.00 from Aberdeen sat till close on midnight before buses could ferry them through the floods. By Thursday, Queen Street was back in business, the trains splashing through the puddles in the tunnels.

## The Fairy Palace

An 'almost fairy palace—furnished with a beautiful passengers' parade on each side, covered in by a roof supported on forty-eight columns, arranged in double rows' was how an 1842 guide book saw Queen Street. In no time at all, however, goblins had ousted the fairies and played tricks with every engineer and architect who crossed their path. Lack of space, company rivalry, a boom in traffic and a temperamental incline plagued Victorian Queen Street. Though the NB stead-fastly refused to become a patron of the finer aspects of archi-tecture, the precedent had been set by the E&G. In 1841 it had enticed Messrs Scott, Steven & Gale of Glasgow and David Rhind of Edinburgh to plan a grand Euston-type gateway but got cold feet when it realised the cost. As late as 1976. at the corner of West George Street stood a mouldering but graceful classical pile. It was the West George Street Chapel (Wardlaw's Kirk) acquired for £14,000 in 1855 and hurriedly converted into railway offices. Now forgotten are the count-less unexecuted plans to ease traffic operation. Neil Robson's scheme of 1852 assumed that the E&G would be diverted to the Caledonian stronghold at Buchanan Street. Then the E&G would be taken-over by the Caledonian and Queen Street closed. The 1870s brought new proposals, Thomas Bouch and John Strain thought nothing stood in the way of a 2 mile 42yd (3.3km) deviation with '2057 lineal yards [1881m] of tunnel in place of 1060 [969m] as at present'. Then there was James Keyden, a well-known Glasgow solicitor and property specu-lator, who wanted Charles Forman to engineer a Glasgow & Dumbartonshire Railway with a passenger station at Sauchie-hall Street. The NB dropped this idea like a hot potato when it discovered that it would have to give the GDR plots number 5 and 6 on the plans 'which are not required for railway pur-poses' and pay them 'two pence for each passenger using the station and passing to or from Dumbartonshire'. The most dramatic scheme was that of Messrs Simpson & Wilson which was rejected on 12 July 1899. They envisaged a third station on girders and columns 16ft 0in (4.9m) above and at right-angles to High Level, serving a relief line running eastwards and join-ing the Sighthill and Coatbridge branches immediately to the east of Bellgrove Station.

Nevertheless, between 1877 and 1888 much of the present High Level came into being. The tunnel under Cathedral Street and Holmhead Street was widened and opened-up to in-crease platform capacity, and in September 1878 a £17,500 contract was signed with P & W. MacLellan of Glasgow for a new roof (Plate 18). Designed by James Carswell, the NB engineer-in-chief, it is in the form of a glazed tied arch, 450ft 0in × 250ft 0in (107.0m × 76.0m), the greatest height above rail level being 78ft 10in (24.0m). The only one of its size and type left in Scotland, it gives High Level that curious echoing feeling. Lovers of good Victorian architecture will be horrified to learn that in 1960 it was actually proposed that this gem should be demolished in favour of individual canopies over each platform. Carswell introduced on the Glasgow City & District line a novel system for electric lighting of carriages which alleviated the gloom of the underground stations. Adopted in December 1886, this consisted of a live insulated centre rail, which was contacted by a spring-loaded iron pulley underneath each coach. The return was through the running rails. The current used was generated at the High Level power station. There were two incandescent lamps in each compartment, which burned on average for about one hour a day, at a cost of one penny per hour per lamp. The system was fully automatic, switched on and off without attention from the guard or the driver. It was abandoned in November 1901 with the introduction of the conventional (Stone's patent) battery belt-driven generator system.

## The Cowlairs Incline

The Cowlairs incline has dominated the working, and indeed the development, of Queen Street Station. It quickly became one of the busiest sections of the line, and the most dangerous.

On 10 November 1840 the directors announced that Kerr, Neilson & Co. of Glasgow had been given a £2900 contract for building the stationary winding engine at the head of the Cowlairs incline. By May 1841 an order was placed with Heggie & Son of Newcastle for a hemp rope weighing 239 cwt and costing £538–6–3d (£538.32). The incline had its own special superintendent, while its first engineman had previously been employed on the inclined plane of the Edinburgh & Dalkeith Railway.

It is likely that the basic method of operation remained unchanged throughout the period of rope haulage. In 1902 it was as follows. When a train from the east reached Cowlairs, the locomotive was detached and replaced by special brake vehicles (never fewer than two) which weighed from 14 to 15 tons (14.3 to 15.3 tonnes) each. The descent into the station was controlled by these. Shunting and assisting over the top of the incline was done by pilot engines always kept at the ready, but ascending trains and their locomotives, though assisted by the stationary engine, could pass Cowlairs without stopping. Attached to the main cable was a 'messenger' rope connected to a draw hook on the buffer beam of the locomotive (Plate 19). On receiving the all-clear signal from Queen Street the stationary engine was started. It had an indicator reading up to 100 revolutions and told the engineman the exact position of the train on the line. When a train arrived at the top of the incline, the engine was stopped to allow the main rope to slacken, thus allowing the messenger rope to drop off the draw hook. Then the first brakesman disconnected the slip coupling of the brake trucks which were allowed to run of their own momentum forward to the platform, under the control of the second brakesman.

The risks involved in incline working were well known and the E&G was taking no chances; every mishap had to be reported. For example, when the son of a passenger had his watch broken in a train entering Glasgow in July 1842 a special enquiry was ordered. Perhaps the greatest worry was the behaviour of some of the railway employees. Mr Stewart, the station superintendent, was warned 'not to stand on the steps of the carriages while accompanying the trains down the incline'. Mr Paton, superintendent of locomotives, got a more severe reprimand, for while on a descending train he suddenly decided without warning to have one brake van only in operation; there was no mishap. The same cannot be said of a goods train which left Cowlairs at 5.00am on 1 July 1844 with only one brake vehicle for 'from the slight resistance thus opposed to its progress had entered the passenger shed on the second line of rails with such force as to carry the brake and several trucks entirely through the portion of the station house appropriated to the parcel office, and into the passage or carriage way in front of the booking office. There had been only one man on the train who had jumped off in the passenger shed.' Earlier that same year the workshops at Cowlairs had completed 'a locomotive engine of a very powerful description'. It was thought that this would obviate the need for rope haulage. Little is known of the trials of this locomotive, but the evidence suggests that it was not a success. Writing in *The Railway Magazine* for February 1901 J. Calder said that 'no engine ever brings its train into the high level terminus'. This was not always so. As early as 1845 it was suggested that delays at Cowlairs could be removed by using locomotives instead of the special vehicles. Very occasionally locomotives did take their trains down the incline, but quite apart from reasons of safety there was the strong argument that there were no proper facilities for coaling and watering them at Queen Street. The incline provided a convenient excuse for deferring improvements to the station yard and auxiliary sidings.

On 16 February 1847 it was decided to install wire ropes and alter the Neilson engine 'to the extent recommended by the report of Mr McNaught' but this did not prevent a runaway goods train in October demolishing a wall at Queen Street and killing one man. In the following year it was reported that the new machinery could haul up trains of twenty or more carriages, whereas the old installation could only cope with a maximum of twelve or fourteen.

The worst accident on the incline occurred on 1 August 1850, when the Scottish Central Railway (which had running powers between Sighthill and Cowlairs), having underestimated the traffic generated by the Highland and Agricultural Society's cattle show in Glasgow, neglected to tell the E&G

that excursion tickets would be valid on the 6.45am train from Perth. To the already hopelessly overloaded train, three cattle wagons and three sheep trucks were attached at Greenloaning Station to accommodate those who had been riding on the roofs of the carriages. At Bishopbriggs and Cowlairs, signals were disobeyed, and wagons and trucks were smashed to matchwood by an oncoming E&G train. Who was to blame? Two engine drivers, one guard and one porter found themselves on a charge of culpable homicide. On 11 January 1851 *The Scotsman* reported a verdict of not guilty. It was a technical case in the fullest sense, but the business of the cattle trucks and the lack of supervision of minor employees clearly pointed to incompetence in senior management.

Apart from regular renewal of the ropes (see Table 7) the original system remained almost unaltered until rope haulage ended (see below). A second cylinder was added in the 1850s, giving increased power to deal with growing traffic (see Table 5).

**Table 5: Passenger traffic between Glasgow & Edinburgh 1855–62**

| Year | Number of Passengers |
|------|----------------------|
| 1855 | 194,920½ |
| 1856 | 371,773½ |
| 1857 | 252,276 |
| 1858 | 239,102½ |
| 1859 | 226,616¼ |
| 1860 | 227,826 |
| 1861 | 234,052 |
| 1862 | 213,384 |

A bad feature of Cowlairs was the water supply. Locomotive boiler tubes on the E&G had an average life of 50,000 miles compared with the 120,000 of those of Caledonian locomotives. In 1856 it was planned to pipe water from Croy to Cowlairs, but this was turned down when it was found that it would cost £2522. It is incredible in the light of this to read that when the boilers for the stationary engine were renewed in

1858, they were 17 years old and had worked with few repairs and no accidents. In the early 1850s annual expenses of working the incline came to just over £2000. In 1899 the cost was £5000, nearly £1000 of which was spent on wire rope. In 1902 H. Muthesius, technical attaché to the German Embassy, wrote for information on the incline. Jackson's reply (Table 6) was prompt and informative.

**Table 6**

| | |
|---|---|
| Circumference of cable | 5in [127mm] |
| Speed of movement | about 14mph [21kph] |
| Life of cable | about 14 months |
| HP of engine | 650 |
| Average weight of trains (excluding engine and tender) | 200 tons |
| Number of trains per day | 70 to 80 |

He also described the method of working already quoted (page 82), though by that time was contemplating changes.

On 4 January 1901 Jackson had asked the locomotive department whether 'it would be practicable to work the trains up the incline with the assistance in the rear of electric engines or motors'. This was a response to a letter he had received a year before from Bennett & Ward-Thomas, electrical engineers in Manchester, who gave figures purporting to show that whereas a train weighing 100 tons (102 tonnes) would require 30lb of coal per mile (5.1kg/km), the equivalent electrical power required only needed 15lb or 16lb (5.2–5.3kg/km) of coal to generate it. In November 1901 Adam Haddow, a Glasgow tile merchant, wrote to say that the incline 'be treated as a separate line somewhat like the subway, with electric overhead wires to be used for haulage and lighting'. Alexander Kennedy, of 17 Victoria Street, Westminster, made perhaps the most sensible suggestion. The electric locomotives he proposed would be of the double-bogie type, 40ft 0in (12.2m) long, with two motors on each bogie, giving about 250hp each. The power station was to be beside the line at Pinkson, current being picked up by a central steel rail protected by timber

Table 7:    Statistics relating to Cowlairs Incline wire ropes, 1848–1908

| Date installed | Supplied by | Age Years | Days | No. of trains | Weight cwt | qr | lb | Cost £ | s | d |
|---|---|---|---|---|---|---|---|---|---|---|
| Mar 1848 | | 2 | 122 | | | | | | | |
| Jul 1850 | | 2 | 240 | | | | | | | |
| Mar 1853 | | 1 | 334 | | | | | | | |
| Feb 1855 | | 2 | 204 | | | | | | | |
| 23 Aug 1857 | Glass, Elliot & Co | 2 | 40 | | | | | | | |
| 2 Oct 1859 | | 1 | 348 | | | | | | | |
| 15 Sep 1861 | Warrington Wire Co (Steel) | 1 | 254 | | | | | | | |
| 27 May 1863 | | 1 | 44 | | | | | | | |
| 10 Jul 1864 | | 1 | 356 | | | | | | | |
| 1 Jul 1866 | | 1 | 174 | | | | | 595 | 10 | – |
| 22 Dec 1867 | J & E Wright | 1 | 152 | | | | | 572 | 8 | – |
| 23 May 1869 | | 1 | 146 | | | | | 606 | 17 | 8 |
| 16 Oct 1870 | J & E Wright | 1 | 105 | | 481 | 1 | 18 | 606 | 15 | 3 |
| 29 Jan 1872 | J & E Wright | | 334 | | 485 | 2 | 14 | 582 | 15 | – |
| 29 Dec 1872 | J & E Wright | | 315 | | 485 | 1 | 0 | 740 | – | 2 |
| 9 Nov 1873 | J & E Wright | 1 | 118 | | 486 | | 21 | 753 | 11 | 9 |
| 7 Mar 1875 | J & E Wright | 1 | 6 | | 454 | 3 | 11 | 602 | 13 | 6 |
| 13 Mar 1876 | Rylands & Co Ltd | 1 | 33 | | 429 | 1 | 0 | 541 | 18 | 6 |
| 15 Apr 1877 | J & E Wright | | 364 | | 445 | 3 | 0 | 507 | – | 9 |
| 14 Apr 1878 | J & E Wright | | 315 | | 448 | 3 | 14 | 471 | 6 | 4 |
| 23 Feb 1879 | Heggie | 1 | 13 | | 471 | – | – | 439 | 15 | 9 |
| 7 Mar 1880 | Heggie | 1 | 20 | | 466 | – | – | 454 | 7 | – |
| 27 Mar 1881 | Heggie | | 350 | 17,631 | 445 | – | – | 433 | 17 | 6 |
| 12 Mar 1882 | Heggie | | 329 | 19,553 | 439 | – | – | 428 | – | 6 |
| 4 Feb 1883 | Heggie | | 328 | 20,256 | 447 | – | – | 391 | 2 | 6 |
| 16 Nov 1884 | Elliott | | 238 | 14,328 | 430 | 3 | – | 344 | 12 | – |
| 12 Jul 1885 | Heggie | | 217 | 15,604 | 450 | – | – | 382 | 10 | – |
| 14 Feb 1886 | Heggie | | 320 | 18,371 | 457 | – | – | 388 | 9 | – |
| 12 Dec 1886 | Heggie | | 266 | 14,839 | 458 | 3 | – | 389 | 18 | 9 |
| 4 Sep 1887 | Heggie | | 273 | 15,000 | 475 | — | | 391 | 17 | 6 |
| 3 Jun 1888 | Heggie | | 295 | 16,131 | 485 | – | – | 400 | 2 | 6 |
| 24 Mar 1889 | Newall (Lang's Patent) | 1 | 139 | 28,191 | 461 | 1 | 8 | 438 | 5 | 1 |
| 10 Aug 1890 | Newall (Lang's Patent) | 1 | 55 | 24,811 | 463 | 3 | 24 | 440 | 15 | 3 |
| 4 Oct 1891 | Heggie | | 231 | 13,893 | 488 | – | – | 396 | 10 | – |
| 22 May 1892 | Heggie | 1 | 76 | 27,262 | 287 | 2 | – | 396 | 1 | 11 |
| 6 Aug 1893 | Newall | 1 | 132 | 31,569 | 465 | – | 7 | 535 | 19 | 11 |
| 16 Dec 1894 | Newall & Co | 1 | 83 | 28,328 | 489 | – | 25 | 440 | 6 | 0 |
| 8 Mar 1896 | Dixon Corbett and R.S. Newall & Co. | | 6 | 23,598 | 490 | 1 | 14 | 453 | 11 | 11 |
| 14 Mar 1897 | R.S. Newall & Co | 1 | 55 | 26,145 | 473 | 2 | 26 | 461 | 17 | 8 |
| 8 May 1898 | Dixon & Corbett | 1 | 34 | 25,607 | 489 | 2 | – | 440 | 11 | – |
| 11 June 1899 | Heggie | 1 | 125 | 31,647 | 476 | – | – | 452 | 4 | – |
| 14 Oct 1900 | Heggie | 1 | 69 | 27,762 | 482 | 3 | – | 543 | 1 | 11 |
| 22 Dec 1901 | Heggie | 1 | 34 | 24,779 | 485 | – | – | 521 | 7 | 6 |
| 25 Jan 1903 | Heggie | 1 | 48 | 25,906 | 518 | – | – | 511 | 10 | 6 |
| 13 Mar 1904 | Heggie | 1 | 121 | 29,486 | 516 | – | – | 516 | – | – |
| 12 Jul 1905 | Heggie | | 354 | 24,229 | 512 | 2 | – | 576 | 11 | 3 |
| 1 Jul 1906 | Heggie | | 357 | 24,023 | 515 | – | – | 579 | 7 | 6 |
| 23 Jun 1907 | Heggie | | 304 | 17,212 | 487 | 3 | 2 | 487 | 15 | 4 |
| 26 Apr 1908 | Heggie | | | | 485 | 1 | 2 | 436 | 16 | 5 |

Plates 12 and 13. (*Above*) The undercroft of the second Central Station under construction in 1902. Workmen are tiling the façade to Midland Street. (*Below*) Central Low Level Station under construction *circa* 1895. Temporary track is still in use; the wagons are carrying bricks for the side walls and platforms. The construction of the roof, with riveted girders supporting brick arches, is clear. [*Sir William Arrol & Co Ltd; British Rail*]

*Plate 14.* St Enoch Station and Hotel, *circa* 1900, with the Glasgow District Subway Station on the right. [*T. R. Annan & Son*]

guards. He estimated the capital cost at £153,000. In 1906 Siemens Bros were trying to sell their own scheme, but the advocates of steam traction had won the day.

Jackson's first battle was with Matthew Holmes, superintendent of locomotives. Although correct in stating that siding accommodation at Queen Street was limited, Holmes maintained that a minimum of five engines (ie two single-shifted and three double-shifted banking pilots) would be required, whereas Inspector Stewart showed that only four were needed. Holmes was against any modernisation, but Stewart managed to win over Deuchars, superintendent of the line. He showed that without the rope, trains could ascend in two minutes less, the number of men employed would be reduced from 31 to 12 and wages from £2000 to £850. Stewart had examined some English inclines worked by locomotives and had come up with very interesting statistics. (See Table 8.)

Table 8: **Statement showing particulars of gradients and loads on British inclines, 1902**

| Place | Length (yd) | Continuous gradient 1 in | Single locomotive load of passenger vehicles (pairs of wheels) | Speed (mph) |
|---|---|---|---|---|
| Bow Road | 400 | 40 | 18 | — |
| Exeter | 1,188 | 37 | 24 | — |
| (considerable curves and more than half in tunnel) | | | | |
| Plympton | 4,840 | 40–42 | 31 | c33 |
| (two curves—open all the way) | | | | |
| Bromsgrove | 3,960 | 37 | 21 | c23 |
| (dead straight and open) | | | | |
| Cowlairs | 2,090 | 41¼–50 | — | c9 |

It took a near-serious accident to convince the NB management that action was necessary. On 24 January 1902 locomotive No 601 and nine vehicles left Queen Street at 9.12am. It arrived at Cowlairs at 9.18am, but Joseph Beagrie, the engineman, failed to shut off steam and the messenger rope being carried forward proceeded to rip up the battens covering the well under the track which held the driving pulleys. The locomotive driver, thinking that his train had been derailed, then applied the Westinghouse brakes. The two brake vehicles which had already been detached by slip coupling in the usual way as the train had passed the summit of the incline and were running ten yards behind, now dashed into the rear of the standing train. Luckily nobody was seriously injured and No 601 continued to Perth. Beagrie was demoted to fireman, and an engine driver and ticket collector who had been travelling on the brakes without a pass received severe reprimands. Major J. W. Pringle of the Board of Trade had nothing spectacular to say in his report, but this minor accident caused the NB to reconsider the whole subject of incline working.

The expedient eventually adopted was to use heavy steam tank locomotives to assist trains up the incline (see Plate 20), and new regulations covering the working of the incline came into force on 12 December 1907. One of them stipulated that enginemen 'must have a clear fire so that no smoke be perceptible in the tunnel', though by 1909 the smoke had become so bad that drivers could not always see the signals, and following a minor collision these had to be further upgraded. At first there were misgivings about allowing trains to descend under their own brake power, and exhaustive tests were made on the braking capabilities of vehicles. During one on Sunday 16 December 1907 a train weighing 316t 17cwt (323.2 tonnes) had stood 40 minutes secured by the air brake alone.

Eventually on 31 January 1908 the NB finally decided that all passenger trains should be taken from Cowlairs to Queen Street by their own engines, instead of the incline brakes; 'while little or no saving would be effected no additional expense would be involved'. Not till 26 August 1909 was authority given to remove the cable, for James Bell, the company's engineer-in-chief, was very alarmed at the possible effect of locomotive blast on the roof of the tunnel. To abolish the old method of getting into and leaving the depot had taken over ten years of arguments and experiment. The North British was now confident that it was saving £756–12–0 (£756.60) per annum, but modernisation had its casualties. The magnificent stationary engine had recently been repaired. It was suggested that it could now be used to generate electricity for the locomotive workshops, but in September 1909 it was condemned to the scrap heap. The 3 tons (3.1 tonnes) of non-ferrous and 270 tons (275 tonnes) of ferrous scrap, together with the seven boilers and their fittings, were estimated to be worth £1301–12–10d (£1301.69). Some of the brass was cast into souvenir paperweights.

Since October 1976 traffic in the High Level tunnel has run on continuous welded track laid on tailor-made 3-tonne precast pre-stressed concrete ladder units resting on steel-faced concrete blocks. By screwing in bolts between ladder and block the inclination has been adjusted to an accuracy of a few millimetres. Maintenance has been reduced and there is now headroom for electrification. The latest news (May 1978) is more encouraging. All going well, in 1979 the decaying push-pull trains will be replaced by High-Speed Trains air-conditioned coaches hauled by a single class 47 locomotive with a control cabin at the end of each train.

# 5

# BUCHANAN STREET STATION

When the railway was king, it was from Buchanan Street that you escaped to 'romantic and highland' destinations like Stirling, Dunblane, Perth, Crieff, Callander, Dundee, Aberdeen, Inverness and Oban. Buchanan Street was not a busy station like Central or Queen Street—in that sense it was a country terminal. Apart from bursts of traffic at 8.00am, 10.00am, at lunchtime and teatime, there were hours when nothing moved at all. The odour of the place was far from prepossessing—a curious blend of fish and chemicals, with bread predominating. West Highlanders considered Glasgow bread such a great delicacy that specially-fitted bread vans destined for the Oban line regularly haunted the little bay platform on the south-east side of the station. In the early 1950s the dining cars on the West Highland expresses were old converted Pullman cars, faintly recalling the splendours of the Caley's Pullman observation car *Maid of Morvern*. As BR's steam empire dwindled, Gresley A4 streamlined Pacifics gravitated to the Buchanan Street–Aberdeen 3-hour expresses. This was to be their last haunt and, for a time, Buchanan Street was the mecca of the train spotter, though as Professor Jack Simmons reminds us, the station 'was easily the most abominable in Western Europe'. The travelling public had to put up with a small steeply-sloping concourse, a grubby little buffet, and a noisome underground lavatory. From an adjacent goods yard (where stood the largest potato shed in Scotland) came the unremitting clank of shunting. In 1897 the Glasgow press minced no words about the city's 'Gateway to the Highlands':

Of all the ugly blots upon the Glasgow landscape Buchanan Street Railway Station stands easily first. It's an architectural abortion that would raise gall in the heart of an Eskimo; a chemical works or a charnel house is cheerful by comparison. Tenth rate suburban villages have gorgeous buildings erected for the reception of railway travellers; one of the most important railway termini in the greatest municipality on earth is a structure that an Irish pig-keeper would blush to keep his porkers in.

GLASGOW TERMINUS OF THE CALEDONIAN RAILWAY.

Fig 17   Elevation of the proposed Central Station of the Caledonian Railway, 1848. This is the end elevation of the long range fronting the platforms.

This pestiferous duckling was the Caledonian Railway's first real foothold on the north bank, but with the opening of Central Station in 1879 English traffic ceased to use it and consequently it could forget to preen its feathers.

## Early History

In October 1845 the Caledonian board was of the opinion that 'the station proposed by the Clydesdale Junction Company at Argyle Street and Dunlop Street is the best that can be had, and that the station of the Garnkirk Railway at Upper Buchanan Street is to be considered as subordinate at present'. The following year, both these railways had been absorbed by the Caledonian and on 14 October the London architect, William (later Sir William) Tite, was asked to come to Glasgow to prepare plans and elevations of Dunlop Street Station. Tite produced a superb Italianate design (Fig 17), but in a detailed report written in Edinburgh on 27 May 1847 he had nothing to say about stations in Glasgow. What had happened was that the Dunlop Street proposals had sparked off a bitter controversy. An essential part of this scheme as authorised by Parliament in 1846 was a branch from the Polloc & Govan Railway at Gushetfaulds with a bridge across the Clyde, seen by the Clyde Bridges Trust as a threat to its receipts from tolls. On 5 December 1845 the Caledonian directors resolved that 'in the event of no arrangement being entered into . . . to resist *in toto* their demand for compensation in Parliament'. The Glasgow Paisley & Greenock Railway, which for a time had been suspected of making rival claims on the Dunlop Street site, fell into the Caledonian net in 1847. However, the greatest stumbling block turned out to be the Admiralty. In its third half-yearly report dated 26 August 1846, the Caledonian told shareholders that the Dunlop Street scheme had been sanctioned by Parliament but that the bridge required Admiralty approval. The Admiralty in fact would only accept a swing bridge. Brief entries in the company's letter books show a willingness to carry out this requirement, but in the end economic and engineering uncertainties led to the whole project being dropped. For a time (15 February 1848–1 June 1849) Townhead on the old GG&C Railway handled all the English Caledonian traffic (Fig 18). By 10 July 1848 there were daily express

94

# CALEDONIAN RAILWAY.

## ADDITIONAL ACCOMMODATION,
### BY SPECIAL TRAINS,
BETWEEN
## EDINBURGH AND GLASGOW,
### WITHOUT INTERMEDIATE STOPPAGES.

Commencing on MONDAY, July 10, 1848.

| FROM EDINBURGH. | | | | FROM GLASGOW. | | | |
|---|---|---|---|---|---|---|---|
| Trains Leave at | | | Arrive at | Trains Leave at | | | Arrive at |
| 8  0 A.M. | - | - | 10  0 A.M. | 8  0 A.M. | - | - | 10  0 A.M. |
| 11  0 „ | - | - | 1  0 P.M. | 11  0 „ | - | - | 1  0 P.M. |
| 4 30 P.M. | - | - | 6 30 „ | 4 15 P.M. | - | - | 6 15 „ |
| 8  0 „ | - | - | 10  0 „ | 8 30 „ | - | - | 10 30 „ |

### Greenwich Time.

Fares--First Class, 4s.; Second Class, 3s.; Third Class, 2s. 6d.

Conveyances will ply between the Glasgow Station at St Rollox and the Glasgow Joint Railway Station at Bridge Street, for the accommodation of Passengers to and from the West of Scotland.
For the Regulations as to Luggage, &c., see the Company's General Time Bill.

By Order,

### J. W. CODDINGTON, Secretary.

Peter Brown, Printer, Edinburgh.

Fig 18  Handbill advertising Caledonian Railway services between Edinburgh and Glasgow, in competition with the Edinburgh & Glasgow Railway. Note the reference to Greenwich Mean, as opposed to local time, and the road link between St Rollox and Bridge Street.

trains from this station, known as St Rollox, to Edinburgh, with cabs providing connections with Joint Line services at Bridge Street. With the completion of the Clydesdale Junction Railway, the Polloc & Govan Railway was linked to the Caledonian main line at Motherwell, and from 1 June 1849 English services were using a temporary terminus on the South bank at Gushetfaulds. Known as Southside Station, it had been opened on 27 September 1848 to handle the traffic of the Glasgow Barrhead & Neilston Direct Railway. In October 1848 Joseph Locke felt Southside inadequate, and in January 1849 the contract for new buildings was put out to tender. As with Dunlop Street, the architect was William Tite. The new

95

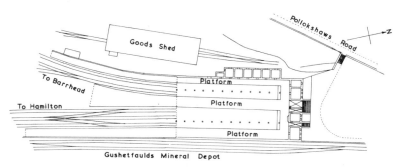

Fig 19   Plan of Southside Station, 1860.

Fig 20   Sketch of Southside Station, c1860, from a photograph.

buildings were somewhat cramped in layout, though the façade was impressive (Figs 19, 20). Behind this there were two pairs of platforms, partly covered, one pair each for the Barrhead and Hamilton trains. The Tite building was demolished in 1873 to make a connection between the Barrhead and City Union Lines, though temporary provision was made for passengers until the construction of links from Strathbungo and Gushetfaulds to Eglinton Street and thence to Bridge Street and Central stations in 1879.

Although the branch to Buchanan Street had been authorised in 1847, there were still serious engineering and political difficulties. For a time it was referred to as the 'Garnkirk Station' for this extension had originally been planned by the GG&C Railway on a steep inclined plane requiring rope

96

haulage. The E&G's problems at Cowlairs (Chapter 4) were a warning to all, and on 28 July 1847 the shareholders were informed of Locke and Errington's solution, which was a branch leaving Milton Junction near Provanmill. Two miles (3.2km) long on a gradient of 1 in 80, it required deep cuttings and 400yd (366m) of tunnel under St Rollox and the Forth & Clyde Canal, which was partly diverted during construction, by coffer dams. By 26 August 1848 three-quarters of the tunnel had been completed. The GG&C had actually built some arching for its inclined plane at a cost of £20,000 and this had to be removed. South of St Rollox the line passed above part of the E&G Queen Street tunnel, and to reduce dangerous overloading on its crown, part of the retaining walls in the Caledonian cutting were built with relieving arches. In December 1847 no immediate capital was available for starting this work and it was believed that there was 'now no hope of the engineer of the Edinburgh & Glasgow coming to terms'. In June 1848 the Caledonian complained that its rival 'had adopted every device to throw difficulties in its way'. Writing from Edinburgh on 21 June, John Errington stated that the final bill for the branch would be in the region of £80,000. Alteration of the levels near the bridge carrying Dobbies Loan over the line had required a payment of £1500 to the Magistrates of Glasgow. However, the 1847 Bill had said nothing about the width of the roadway. The city now accused the railway of illegally reducing it from 50ft 0in to 25ft 0in (15.2m to 7.6m).

In spite of all these difficulties, the new terminal was officially opened to passenger traffic on 1 November 1849.

### Exit William Tite

Tite had first offered his professional advice to the Caledonian Railway in July 1846. On 23 November the directors received plans and elevations of buildings for the Lothian Road Terminal in Edinburgh. As constructed, this was a rather modest affair, but less of a disappointment than Buchanan Street. The contractors for the iron roof at Lothian Road were Fox, Henderson & Co of Renfrew. On 6 August 1850 Tite had been asked to inquire as to whether or not this firm would be prepared to use spare portions of the Edinburgh roof at Glasgow, but nobody was willing to meet the cost of substantial buildings. Worse still, in January 1850 Tite's architectural fees amounted to £6181–8s–3d (£6181.42) of which only £2024–18s–6d (£2024.92½) had been paid. When he asked for the balance of £4156–1s–6d (£4156.7½) still due, in a letter dated 2 September 1850 the company, then suffering from a serious cash crisis, replied that it could not make an exception in his case. Philip Hardwick, architect to the London & Birmingham Railway, interceded on Tite's behalf, and in January 1851 the dispute was remitted to a 'Glasgow architect of standing'. Reluctantly, the Caledonian allowed its solicitor to let the case go to the Court of Session, which on 4 February 1851 pronounced in Tite's favour. The company was allowed to deduct £16–19s–0d (£16.95) being an acknowledged overstatement of Fox, & Henderson's account, on which Tite's commission had been calculated.

Tite's departure like the abandonment of the monumental gateway at Queen Street (Chapter 4) was symptomatic of the change in mood at this time. Inflation hit the over-optimistic and under-capitalised railway companies hard in the 1850s. At least from 19 October 1850 passengers at Buchanan Street and Lothian Road Stations could see 'a board showing the arrival and departure of trains'. In September 1858 the buildings at Buchanan Street were whitewashed for £18–0s–0d—it was the admission of another architectural failure. In 1858 the passenger station (Plate 21, Fig 21) appears to have had one short and one long platform, with a small bay and an 'end-loading facility'. There were the usual small turntables to transfer 4-wheeled coaches between running lines, and a long, narrow block of 'booking offices'. The whole sorry affair was sandwiched between the very much larger goods station, and soap and chemical works.

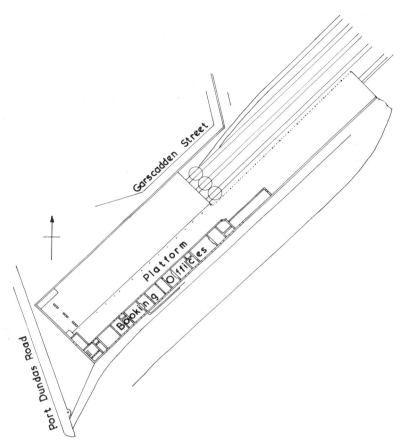

Fig 21   Plan of Buchanan Street Station, 1860, showing the building illustrated in Plate 21.

## The Architectural Competition of 1857–1858 and its Aftermath

The Caledonian Railway (Crofthead Extension and Amendment) Act 1853 had authorised the construction of an hotel at Buchanan Street. This was a challenge to the E&G's establishment in George Square, but the hotel was never built. Then on 4 November 1857 the company announced a competition for plans of a proposed new passenger station and offices, the premiums not exceeding £200 in all. On 7 April 1858 it was reported that a committee had

> received 63 designs—of these many of the most elegant were reluctantly rejected as the cost of their erection would have far exceeded the sum to which the competitors were limited, others were at once put aside on account of their arrangements being defective. The remaining plans were carefully examined by your committee, assisted by Mr Charles Wilson, architect, whom they consulted with regard to technical difficulties, and they report the directors to award.

Wilson received a fee of ten guineas (£10.50). First prize went to J. T. Rochead of Glasgow, who was later to design the fantastic baronial Wallace Monument at Stirling. The fact that he had used the motto 'Caledonian Romana' may have accounted for his success. Second prize went to James Collie. Although his plans bore the motto 'Abracadabra', it is not known if they represented a new version of the highly successful classical theme earlier carried out by him at Bridge Street Station. Third in the competition were plans signed 'Signal'. The architect was John Clayton of Hereford who promptly and successfully requested their return. William Burn, the Edinburgh architect who had left for London in 1850, had a dazzlingly successful career. He was responsible for over 700 major buildings in Britain—but his designs for Buchanan Street were rejected, probably because he had supported Tite in his quarrel with the company. Still, no major reconstruction was to be carried through. In any case, as long ago as 1852 the Caledonian had accepted but mothballed the plans of the Glasgow architect James Salmon who naturally felt aggrieved. Remembering the Tite episode, the company decided on a quick cash payment or to 'refer to an arbiter not an architect'.

The outcome was that the design of the station buildings and company's headquarters was left to the discretion of the Caledonian engineers. In 1867 and 1869 the Edinburgh architects,

J. M. Wardrop and Peddie & Kinnear, submitted reports—they remained dead letters. There was also a scheme to have grand new administrative offices on land at Blythswood Holm. Great Glasgow architects including John Burnet and Alexander Thomson were consulted, but the scheme was indefinitely postponed. It was George Graham, the Caledonian's engineer-in-chief, who was to really set the seal on the future development of Buchanan Street; the adjacent goods terminal to the south was to be expanded enormously while the passenger station could be written-off as a lost cause. Nevertheless, until the opening of Central Station, alterations had to be made to cope with increasing traffic. In July 1862 the arrival platform and canopy were lengthened at a cost of £238, and 'to guard against accidents' in the following year £270 was spent in raising the parapet wall at Dobbies Loan. The largest extension was made between 1865 and 1869 so that from 1 January 1870 the station could handle trains from Stirling and the north. Although the Scottish Central and Scottish North Eastern Railways had fallen to the Caledonian in 1865 and 1866, Perth and Aberdeen trains had had to use Queen Street Station where there was a Caledonian booking office. At first sight, it is rather surprising that this arrangement did not often lead to open war, but it is often forgotten that until the opening of their Glasgow and Coatbridge line on 2 January 1871, all NB trains from Coatbridge, Airdrie and beyond trundled to and from Buchanan Street. The alterations of 1865–9 were not dramatic. An exit was constructed at Parliamentary Road and £300 was spent in raising the platforms from 12in to 25in (0.3 to 0.6m). When it came to acquiring land the company was more cautious. Not that it did not have the land, but it was at Blythswood Holm and therefore useless. In January 1870 there were complaints that the station was in 'an untidy condition', but in October George Graham would do nothing until he had improved the goods station. This was still unfinished in 1878. At least there was one ray of hope; on 29 November 1881 the order went out to install arc lamps at both depots. By 1882 passengers could avail themselves of a refreshment room—this had been proposed in 1858, then turned down.

## Buchanan Street at the Turn of the Century

From the 1890s the architectural and engineering feats at Central Station and on the Glasgow Central Railway gave the Caledonian a reputation second to none. Buchanan Street passenger station became a poor relation, with traffic figures relatively static. In 1897 the total number of passengers booked was 808,252; by 1902 this had dropped to 775,569, but in 1908 it was 1,104,971. At the corner of Buchanan and Germiston Streets travellers passed an unimposing 4-storey tenement block, from which the Caledonian ran its empire. Behind this was a huge goods station (Figs 22, 29). The passenger station was to the north. It had only five platforms, the longest being numbers 2 and 3, 702ft 0in and 655ft 0in (214.0m and 200.0m) respectively. They were the only ones which terminated in front of a really narrow concourse, hemmed in on all sides by narrow waiting rooms and offices. Platform 5 was the shortest at 405ft 0in (133.0m), totally uncovered; it was used for milk traffic, but could be pressed into service during rush periods. The low roof over platforms 2 and 3 had the dubious distinction of being carried on 69 wooden posts, each 9in (0.2m) square. The train information board (Plate 23) did not match up to that at Central Station. There were only two lines in the tunnel between St Rollox and Buchanan Street. These served both goods and passenger requirements. Fortunately, the station had little suburban traffic and the main line was normally controlled by a manual box of 98 levers in the station itself, assisted by a box at St Rollox. During holiday periods trains were often double-headed, though owing to lack of space pilot engines were usually detached at Milton Road Junction. Especially during the annual Glasgow Fair holiday crowds surged dangerously on platforms 15ft 9in (4.8m) wide, and in July 1902 a certain James Massie who was seeing friends

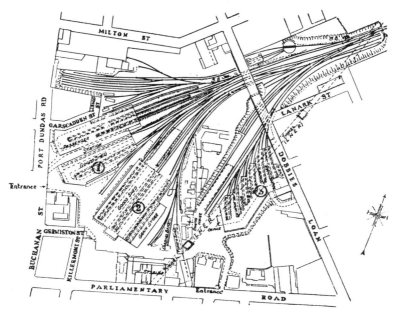

# GLASGOW — BUCHANAN STREET GOODS STATION

## SCALE

Fig 22   Plan of Buchanan Street goods and passenger stations, c1920.

off for Aberdeen was pushed beneath the departing train. His demise resulted in an unsuccessful court action against the company, which claimed there was no need to shut the platform gates. However, in giving evidence, a guard admitted that a large crowd would be over the top of them and that one could not compare Buchanan Street with a modern station. By 1904, however, there had been other accidents, and £215 was immediately spent on extending the platforms between the milk bank and docks numbers 1–4. Various other minor alterations were made up to the outbreak of World War I, but the real opportunity had been lost in 1905. In that year an extension was planned on the site of the old Glasgow City Poorhouse, but in the end the decision rested with the engineers—they opted for a large and enormously expensive warehouse and potato shed

103

at Dobbies Loan. Improvement of the passenger station was eventually undertaken by the LMS in 1932, when the steel-framed glazed awnings from Ardrossan North Station were re-erected, and a new steel-framed, though still wood-clad, concourse was provided. In this form the station had something of the charm of a country terminus (Plates 22–4).

## Buchanan House

Rationalisation in the Beeching era brought closure, on 7 November 1966, quickly followed by demolition. Traffic is now handled at Queen Street. We are happy to record that on the site of the carriage sidings work had already begun in November 1965 on the construction of a 10-storey office block. Known as Buchanan House, it cost over £1.25 million and was the largest block of its kind in Scotland, when opened on 14 December 1967 by the retiring chairman of British Rail. The 600 guests could admire the electronic data processing equipment, the mobile racking in the stationery stores or take a trip to the fourth floor to find wall-to-wall carpeting in the typing centre where there is a mural consisting of a giant type-writer with pictures of pop and jazz stars. With a total floor area of 210,000 sq ft (19,409m²), Buchanan House is no ordinary speculation, for at the outset it was purpose-built as the headquarters of British Rail, Scottish Region. Held on a 125-year lease, it has increased efficiency and economy by enabling the long overdue removal from scattered and outdated office premises in Edinburgh and Glasgow. Glasgow's 'slum terminal' has therefore made amends for its former sins.

Plates 15 and 16. (Above) The concourse at St Enoch Station, circa 1955.
This shows how little the station had been altered since construction. (Below)
Trains awaiting departure from St Enoch Station, 1960. The motive power –
a Fairburn 2–6–4T, a Fowler Class 2P 4–4–0, and a Jubilee 4–6–0 – was
typical of the station in the 1950s and early 1960s. The wooden structure on
the platforms led to an exit for passengers and parcels in Dunlop Street.
[British Rail; John R. Hume]

Plates 17 and 18. (*Above*) Queen Street Station *circa* 1860. On the left is part of 'Wardlaw's Kirk', and the background is the boarded end of the 'almost fairy palace' of 1842. (*Below*) The new overall roof at Queen Street, *circa* 1880. Note the van traffic on the right. [*Strathclyde Regional Archives; P. & W. MacLellan*]

# 6

# SUBURBAN STATIONS—
# A BRIEF SURVEY

Like London, Glasgow experienced a boom in suburban railway construction in the late nineteenth century. On 24 October 1885, *The Builder* in its report on the construction of the Glasgow City & District Railway noted:

> Recent and existing conditions of railway enterprise in Glasgow may, in some sort, be likened to those which in London, twenty years ago, culminated in the construction of the Metropolitan Railway from the Great Western metals to Farringdon Street, and subsequently led to a piercing of the Metropolis in other directions.

In both cities the west experienced suburban growth, but whereas the eastward flow of the Thames kept industrial development away from the west, in its westward course to the Atlantic the Clyde attracted docks and warehouses 'separated by a slight fringe of ship-building territory only from the fashionable residential suburbs'. Unlike London, the north side of Glasgow had no passenger line coming in direct from the west though the GC&DR line, opened in March 1886, connected the east and west; the NB system by a direct underground line connected a reconstructed College Station and Stobcross. Although much of the solid cutting had been 'through an excellent freestone which answered admirably for much of the heavy masonry required along the line', elsewhere the contractors 'experienced no little difficulty with certain subsoils of a more or less treacherous consistency, composed of mixed shifting of softly running sand and mud in combination with water'. While the GC&D Bill was going through Parliament in 1881–2, the NB mooted another underground line, which was subsequently withdrawn. This was the Glasgow City & Dumbartonshire Railway which was to leave its Stobcross line near the Caledonian station at Partick, proceed eastwards, in an S-bend pass under Buchanan Street and Queen Street stations, then run parallel with the GC&D to College. The Caledonian became so alarmed that in December 1881 it toyed with the idea of a duplicate line slightly to the north with stations at Stobcross, Great Western Terrace, Kelvinside Church, Woodside, and Gladstone Street, and Buchanan Street. The Glasgow Central Railway, authorised in 1888, was in the event the Caledonian's solution to tapping northern and western suburban traffic. The solution was drastic—6.25 miles (10.1km) of underground line with stations at Dalmarnock, Bridgeton Cross, Glasgow Green, Glasgow Cross, Central Low Level, Anderston Cross, Stobcross, Kelvin Bridge, Botanic Gardens, Kirklee, Maryhill and Dawsholm. With the opening of the Lanarkshire & Dumbartonshire Railway in October 1896 the link between Dumbarton and Rutherglen was complete. The Cathcart District Railway authorised in 1880 was another Caledonian scheme to exploit the expanding southern suburbs. Although not an underground line, much of the 2.25-mile (3.6km) stretch from the Central Station lines at Pollokshields East to Cathcart was in cutting. It did not open until May 1886. So successful was this venture that by 1894 the line had been extended round by Shawlands, rejoining itself at Pollokshields. Trains on the 'outer circle' ran via Queens Park and Mount Florida, those on the 'inner circle' via Maxwell Park and Pollokshaws East. All 10 stations had island platforms. On the opening day of the extension 89 trains were run both ways giving a 10-minute service from 8.00am to 8.00pm and a 20-minute service before and after these hours. Perhaps the station-masters at Shawlands got the worst deal for their houses were built in the arches of a viaduct. The general superintendent of the line thought the 10-minute service a splendid achievement, but ominously warned that 'it would be a very difficult problem to work out, in view of the crowded condition of Central Station'.

## The Decline of Suburban Services after 1901

What many English contemporaries did not appreciate was that for the majority of Glaswegians, suburbia as we know it today did not exist. This was the city whose centre had the highest population density in Western Europe (Introduction). Even the middle class suburbs such as Langside, Pollokshields, Kelvinside and Hillhead were not more than three miles from the city centre. The electrification of the Glasgow Corporation tramways, begun in 1898, was the death blow to inner-suburban rail services, although three years before, a decrease in traffic receipts on the Cathcart District Railway had prompted the *Glasgow Evening News* to dedicate a Rabbie Steam Burns ode to boardroom speculators.

> We'll be happy by-and-bye
> So, shareholders, do not sigh
> But join with one in choruses of Hope
> If it seems quite necessary
> That our plans we still should vary
> With the Tramway competition for to cope.

When the Caledonian's general manager got his engineers in 1904 to map the tramways in operation, the results were gloomy. Within a 2-mile radius of St Enoch Station, there was a web of tram routes, and from near Pollokshields East Station the Corporation was planning a 2-mile (3.2km) stretch southwards which would be doubled back to form a Cathcart tramway circle. In 1901 and 1903 the Burgh of Clydebank tramways had been taken over by the city fathers. Govan still owned its tram routes, but they were operated by the city.

The statistics were even more depressing:

**Table 9:** Operating statistics for Caledonian Railway suburban stations, 1900–11

| Station | Year | Passengers booked | Coaching receipts (£) |
|---|---|---|---|
| Kelvinbridge | 1897 | 372,724 | 3,159 |
| | 1908 | 73,995 | 1,121 |
| Gushetfaulds | 1897 | 76,360 | 1,369 |
| | 1907 | 10,386 | 250 |
| Botanic Gardens | 1900 | 109,429 | 1,455 |
| | 1911 | 11,036 | 646 |
| Dawsholm | 1900 | 55,038 | 448 |
| | 1907 | 13,411 | 199 |

Taking inner suburban routes, we find that between 1907 and 1917 two Caledonian and five North British stations were permanently closed to passengers; a further eight were temporarily shut as a wartime economy measure. Tramway competition was, however, no new phenomenon: in the 1870s the Glasgow & Paisley Joint Line was already taking a hard look at its services in the face of competition from the Vale of Clyde Tramway's link with Govan. Despite protests, from 31 January 1874 to 1 March 1880, Govan Station only handled workmen's trains.

The same company (following a letter from a certain Mr John Laing) had opened a new station to passenger traffic at Cardonald on 1 September 1879 but only after 'receiving a guarantee of 40 season tickets at £5 each'. By the late 1890s the NB was especially prone to stipulations of this sort. The wealthy suburb of Milngavie fared better. In August 1896 it was decided to double the line and reconstruct the station for not only would it 'stimulate the building operations' but if nothing were done, the residents 'will just set about stirring up a movement for the Caledonian Company coming into the district'. This last consideration gave the 32 season-ticket holders at Hillfoot Terrace 1.5 miles (2.4km) south of Milngavie a station of their own, but ostensibly it was the honouring of a vague promise made by the company in 1888. Nevertheless Mr Douglas, the principal landowner, was unsuccessful in getting the station named Ferguston after his estate. The local Douglas Golf Links seemed a convenient alternative, until it was pointed out that several Caledonian depots were called Douglas, including Douglas Park Colliery.

These additional facilities were only provided in the face of firm evidence of growing demand. In July 1884 there were 13 trains daily to and from Milngavie, but by July 1896 there were 24. The convenience of railway travel led a deputation from Bearsden to demand in February 1896 a new train leaving Queen Street at 3.30pm for schoolchildren and 'for ladies who have been in town shopping and visiting'. They also requested that the 7.40pm train from Milngavie 'be put forward 20 minutes or so to accommodate parties wishing to attend concerts, theatres and the like in Glasgow'. Nearer the city centre, the occupants of Lauderdale Gardens in 1912 got a new access bridge and booking office at Hyndland Station, but were warned that this facility would be withdrawn if additional traffic were not forthcoming.

So serious had tramway competition become that from 1907 to 1915 there was a pooling agreement covering the issue of workmen's tickets from the Dumbarton and Balloch Joint Line to certain Glasgow stations, excluding Rutherglen. Owing to errors made by booking clerks at this station, the NB suspected the Caley of improperly excluding certain receipts from the pool. There were heated exchanges between Jackson and Donald Matheson, but this was nothing when we examine the earlier attempts of the NB and G&SW to run 'bus trains' between St Enoch and Springburn. These services would provide a valuable connection with main line trains at Bellgrove. It was also seen as a trial of strength with the tramways. By January 1899 St Enoch, Queen Street and Alexandra Park fares had been revised from 2½d (1p) first-class single to 2d (1p), and third-class single from 1½d (½p) to one penny (0.5p) but by then both railway and public confidence had

111

been lost. Although the 'bus trains' were being regularly advertised in 1897 as a half-hourly service with mutual availability of tickets, during busy holiday periods the G&SW frequently chose to withdraw them at only a moment's notice. Protests and excuses flowed from both sides, but the public was less patient. *The Glasgow Herald* warned: 'even railway companies, like more humble concerns, cannot afford to treat their regular patrons in so cavalier a manner' and one gentleman writing under the pseudonym *Locomotive* suggested that 'those season ticket holders who were prevented from getting home to dinner should send a debit note for dinner expenses

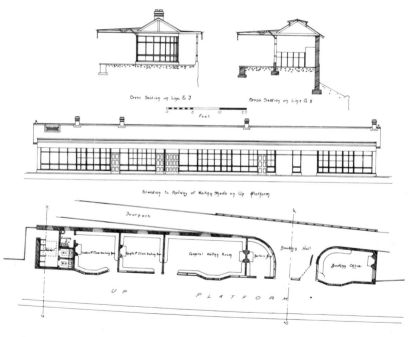

Fig 23   Plan, elevation and sections, up platform building, Partick (now Partickhill) Station, 1886, showing the construction of a wood and brick North British Railway modular station building. The accommodation is typical of suburban stations.

and car fares incurred.' Nor could the companies arrive at a satisfactory pooling agreement. The G&SW pointed to Section 22 of the City of Glasgow Union Railway Partition Act of 1896 which allowed it to claim 33½ per cent working expenses. Yet this was the smaller company inevitably attracted, as the NB quietly admitted in 1897, to 'more remunerative traffic'.

## The Architecture of Suburban Stations

Generally speaking, suburban architecture on the NB was undistinguished, but adequate. A modular design of wooden building was widely used on the new suburban lines opened after 1880, though variations between stations were numerous. A typical example was at Jordanhill (erected 1895) with down and up platforms 12ft 0in (3.7m) wide and respectively 61ft 10in and 79ft 7in (18.9 and 24.3m) long, with wooden buildings founded on one foot square (0.09m²) section wooden piles. Partickhill (Fig 23) was slightly grander. Yorkhill, opened in 1886, was one of the most unattractive, with narrow box-like buildings on an embankment. The suburban termini were better served. College Station, terminus for trains from the east until 1886, was opened in 1871 without covered platforms, using part of the old University buildings for offices, but on 25 July 1872 a contract was let for an iron-roofed train shed at a cost of £8389 (Figs 24, 25). The roof trusses had a span of 76ft 10½in (23.4m), and the shed was 150ft 0in (45.8m) long. Hyndland (opened 1886) had an imposing two-storey block at street level, with stairs down to spacious canopied platforms.

Bridgeton Central Station, opened in 1892 when Caledonian competition in eastern Glasgow was beginning to take effect, though not noteworthy architecturally, had good glazed awnings over the platforms. The outer suburban terminus at Milngavie, originally a modest masonry structure, had an elaborate awning added in 1899 for £1471. A Blyth & Cunningham idea for a 'double verandah' roof 520ft (158.5m) long, to cost £5000, was rejected, a typical NB decision.

113

FRONT OF OLD COLLEGE, NOW A RAILWAY STATION.

Fig 24  Sketch of old Glasgow College (Glasgow University) buildings converted to offices for College Station. The gateway shown here was dismantled when the building was demolished, and re-erected in 1886 as part of what is known as Pearce Lodge at the new University at Gilmorehill. The removal was financed by Sir William Pearce, managing director of the Fairfield Shipyard, and was executed by Messrs Morrison & Mason.

Fig 25  Sketch of College Station, passenger side, in 1970.

114

Fig 26   Sketch of the surface building at Botanic Gardens Station as built.
The platforms were wholly underground.

Caledonian stations were generally superior in style to those
of the NB. The wooden stations on the Cathcart District line
opened 1886–94 were above average, and most are still in use.
They were all on island platforms, a successful innovation
which reduced staff costs and gave effective control of passenger flow. Island platforms were also used on some of the stations on the Glasgow Central Railway, and exclusively on the
Lanarkshire & Dumbartonshire. On the latter, steel framing
was extensively adopted, giving an airy appearance to the stations. The Glasgow Central stations made up by architectural
elegance—they were described as 'for the most part pic-
turesque'—for the somewhat stygian conditions below ground
(Plate 26). The stations were almost all poorly ventilated,
which at rush hours could result in choking concentrations of

sulphur dioxide. J. J. Burnet, James Miller and Robert Wemyss designed some charming buildings (see also Chapter 9). An article on the architecture of Glasgow in *The Builder* of 9 July 1898 wrongly attributed 'The Botanical Gardens Station of the Caledonian Railway' to J. J. Burnet (it was a Miller product, Fig 26) but described it as 'a pretty little red brick tiled building, with white woodwork and half-timber gables, a strange sight in Glasgow; it has two tall turrets on the roof with gilded onion-shaped domes, is very well grouped and detailed, and looks too good architecturally for what it is.' Burnet's best were probably Kelvinside (Fig 27), Glasgow Cross (Plate 25) and Kirklee, and Wemyss was responsible for the Maryhill Station, the drawings for which were prepared in the office of Formans & McCall, civil engineers.

Fig 27  Sketch of the surface building of Kelvinside in 1968. Behind this façade twin staircases descended to the platforms, which were in cutting.

A Caley suburban station of a more modest type, Robroyston, was designed by Donald Matheson in 1898. It had platforms 94ft 0in and 44ft 0in (28.7 and 13.4m) long, with Staffordshire terra-metallic chequered paving. The wooden buildings were in Swiss chalet style (also found on the NB West

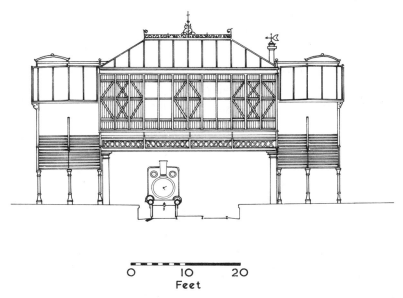

O      IO      2O
Feet

Fig 28   Elevation of the Glasgow & South Western Railway booking office at Shields Road Station, 1884. This building was designed for the opening of the 'Canal Line' (see also Plate 28).

Highland line), roofed with Aberfoyle slates and red terracotta ridge tiles. The canopies were supported on ornamental cast-iron brackets. The estimated cost of this little station was £4319, later increased to £4356.

The Glasgow & South Western had few suburban stations of its own. Services on the Glasgow & Kilmarnock and Glasgow & Paisley joint lines were shared with the Caley, but the G&SW built new stations for the opening of the Paisley (Canal) route in 1885, at Shields Road, Bellahouston, Corkerhill (for railwaymen only) and Crookston. The two first-named had pleasing wooden buildings in chalet style, with cast-iron cresting, the elevated booking office at Shields Road (Fig 28) costing £2699–7s–2d (£2699.36). Crookston has a particularly charming stone building, with a decorative wooden screen (Plate 28). More imposing was the company's Eglinton Street (later Cumberland Street) station of

117

1899–1900, designed by William Melville to compete with a new Caley station of best Matheson/Miller style. The G&SW station had art nouveau and renaissance details on the red-sandstone-faced street frontages.

The tramway competition encountered after 1900 effectively halted the development of new suburban routes, but post-World War I housing development did result in the erection of new stations at King's Park and Croftfoot on the former Lanarkshire & Ayrshire Railway. These were in the Matheson/Miller tradition, though without the lightness of touch of these designers. More recently, the creation of the giant Drumchapel housing estate resulted in the opening of a new station at Drumry, with utilitarian red-brick buildings. During the past few years many of the surviving suburban stations have had their buildings replaced by steel-and-glass structures, offering minimal accommodation, but presenting a smaller target to vandals.

### Westerton Station—a Case Study

Westerton Station is situated at the junction of the former Glasgow & Milngavie Junction Railway with the Glasgow, Dumbarton & Helensburgh Railway; it is 4½ miles (7.2km) from the city centre. The G&MJR was incorporated in 1861 and merged into the NB in 1873; however, until 1913 there was no station at Westerton, only a farm of that name. The whole area was following the familiar pattern, the increasing drive westwards was making it part of Greater Glasgow, but the initiative for a station did not come from the railway company.

Although in 1911 Glasgow was first and foremost a city violently pursuing the Scottish tenement tradition, in May of that year the NB received a letter from a Mr M. Boyd Auld, the legal representative of a society, with proposals 'to form a garden suburb on part of the Garscube Estate which adjoins the NB system at the branch to Bearsden'. Auld reckoned that this development would house some 300 families but the 'proposal depends entirely on whether or not a station is built'. As it turned out, the Glasgow Garden Suburb Tenants Ltd, which was registered under the Friendly Societies Acts on 16 August 1912, was a housing society catering almost exclusively for telegraph clerks and engineers in the Post Office, but since the philosophy of the garden suburb movement was alien to Glasgow, Auld had to get assistance from the London town planning consultant Sir Raymond Unwin.

On 19 April 1913 at 3.00pm a special train arrived from Queen Street so that Lady Campbell, in the presence of Earl Grey and other notables, could lay the foundation stone of the development. By 24 May 1913 the first tenants were in occupation, yet the station was only opened for coaching, goods, and mineral traffic on 1 August.

It had taken Auld a lot of patient negotiation to achieve this. In June 1911, W. F. Jackson, the NB general manager, had got the following opinion from Donald Deuchars, superintendent of the line:

> The building of this suburb would probably result in the tramway being attracted to it, and we would find from experience, as we have found elsewhere, that for short distances, our trains cannot successfully compete with the tramways. Besides, it has been found necessary to close stations on the outskirts of our large cities, and for these reasons therefore, I could not recommend the erection of a station.

The Anniesland tram terminus at Great Western Road was within a half-mile (0.8km) of the Forth & Clyde Canal at Temple; it would only take another half-mile (0.8km) to reach the north-east end of the garden suburb. By 13 November 1912 work had started on erecting a station, but since the total cost was estimated at £3368, the NB not unnaturally required the promoters to guarantee an annual sum of £650 against running losses.

In December Auld was informed that the new station might be called 'Garscube', after the name of the estate on which the suburb is situated—in the end both agreed that 'Garden Suburb' was the nicer-sounding alternative. New signalling was necessary at Milngavie Junction, Bearsden Station and Knightswood North Junction. The station (Plate 29) was a modest wooden building with a standard NB drinking fountain, and a porters' room. The last was only installed after complaints that the porters were likely to make a bothy of the booking office, but since there were no shops in the vicinity 'the probability is that there will be a good deal of parcels traffic to deal with, which will be stored in the booking office for periods'. Electric light was to be installed at a capital cost of £70, the annual running cost being £19–18s–0d (£19.90), but for some time the Westerton commuters had to make do with oil lamps.

The question of draining the station and agent's house created friction between the NB and Auld. The suburb was to provide 'reasonable drainage facilities' but the county council stipulated that the sewer must pass through the goods yard. The NB opposed this, and on 9 April 1913 told a furious Auld that he would have no station unless he could find a drainage outlet. Four days later there emerged a compromise acceptable to all: by taking the sewer across the Helensburgh line and carrying it westward along the south side of the railway, the goods yard could be avoided. There were other problems too. Construction work was held up, for until 13 May 1913 the draft title deeds to the ground had not been approved. Moreover that same day the railway refused to form the footpath and curves to the station square. It had also made a bureaucratic muddle by calling the new station 'Westernton' though on 8 March 1913 both sides had agreed to the present name with 'Garden Suburb' being added to the name boards. It was only on 12 June 1914 that the Board of Trade gave its official blessing to the work. In his report, Major Pringle described the station as comprising an up and a down platform both 200yd (183m) long and 14ft 0in (4.3m) wide. The up platform had a combined general waiting room and booking hall, conveniences, and ladies' room (Plate 29). The down platform had a wooden waiting shed and a Macfarlane's urinal. Apart from a few modifications required to the signalling, he had little else to add.

## The Station in Operation

The outbreak of war in 1914 halted the growth of this suburban paradise. The fashionable middle-class enclave of Bearsden was only a mile to the south, yet the barrier between it and Westerton at the railway junction was inevitably physical as well as social. Most of the tenants had to be at work at either 6.00am, 8.00am or 9.00am, yet this was and is a busy stretch of line. By October 1913 a regular service of workmen's trains was in operation Monday to Friday between 5.25am and 7.08am.

This concession had required considerable agitation on Auld's part for NB officials had privately declared their policy in the following terms: 'If all the Milngavie trains were to be stopped at the Garden City Station there would undoubtedly be strong complaints received from Bearsden and Milngavie people, and in view of the proposed extension of the Glasgow Corporation Tramways in that district, it is very undesirable to do anything that would give a fillip to the agitation.' Many tenants wished to follow the Scottish custom of travelling home to lunch, but the timetables soon put a stop to this: there were virtually no trains in the middle of the day.

The factors which gave birth to Westerton Station are perhaps atypical in the Glasgow context, but the traffic statistics most certainly were not (Table 10).

Table 10:   Operating statistics, Westerton Station, 1914–28

| Half Year Ending | Passengers booked | Receipts (£) |
|---|---|---|
| Jun 1914 | 10125 | 88 |
| Dec 1914 | 11442 | 104 |
| Jun 1918 | 10403 | 152 |
| Dec 1918 | 14177 | 217 |
| Jun 1920 | 19177 | 276 |
| Dec 1920 | 20064 | 339 |
| Jun 1924 | 27869 | 367 |
| Dec 1924 | 29193 | 429 |
| Jun 1928 | 11478 | 160 |
| Dec 1928 | 10978 | 288 |

Cash remitted in respect of goods and minerals fell from £118 in 1914 to £45 in 1928. Westerton might well have gone the way of other suburban stations, but electrification in the 1960s plus the growth of a large housing scheme one mile to the east of Drumchapel has given it a new lease of life. The access has been improved by a pedestrian subway under the Forth & Clyde Canal, and the old wooden up platform buildings were replaced by a modern concrete structure a few years ago.

*Plates 19 and 20. (Above)* An Edinburgh express, with two Holmes 4–4–0s, ascending Cowlairs Incline, *circa* 1900. Note the messenger rope to the main cable, attached to the drawhook, and the guide pulleys in boxes on the left-hand track. *(Below)* One of the Reid 0–6–2Ts built by the NBR for banking service, assisting a train out of Queen Street in 1960. [*Scottish Railway Preservation Society; John R. Hume*]

*Plates 21 and 22. (Above)* Buchanan Street Station, *circa* 1860, from the north. The gloominess of the wooden temporary buildings is evident. The coaches appear to be very early 4-wheelers. *(Below)* The frontage of Buchanan Street as rebuilt in 1932. The tower cranes in the background were working on the construction of Buchanan House. [*Strathclyde Regional Archives; John R. Hume*]

# 7

# THE GLASGOW UNDERGROUND

'You've never lived unless you've been on the Glasgow Underground.'

*Cliff Hanley*

'The Subway' was so much a part of Glasgow life that it is difficult to believe that it has gone. Gone not to dereliction and decay, but to be reincarnated in a modern form, with all the much-talked-about features like interchange stations with British Rail, escalators, and rather less of the familiar 'shoogle' of the cars on the undulating track. The old is never the same as the new, and it seems appropriate to include some of the city's more obscure stations in a book devoted largely to the grand and impressive. Where but in Glasgow could you apparently enter a railway station through a retail draper's establishment, or be assailed by the aroma of kippering fish in the centre of a city? Several of the stations on the Underground were conveniently situated next door to licensed premises, while Copland Road station was specially adapted to handle the crowds for Glasgow Rangers football club's celebrated Ibrox Stadium.

Even in its formation the line had its peculiarities, not least of which was the support of such disparate bodies as Glasgow University Senate and the city's Trades' Council. More obviously odd was the use of cable traction underground. Indeed the Glasgow system was unique in its adoption of this technique for passenger traffic. The conditions in which the line was promoted were, however, perfectly straightforward. By the 1880s Glasgow, the second city of the British Empire, was experiencing serious congestion in the city centre streets, where horse-hauled drays, vans, omnibuses, and hackney carriages competed for road space with the horse trams of the Glasgow Tramway & Omnibus Co. The resulting confusion was made worse by the small number of river crossings. The solution to problems of overground chaos was to go underground. The precedent had already been set by the construction of the Glasgow City & District Railway, opened in 1886. This encouraged the promotion of the Caledonian-sponsored Glasgow Central Railway, which like the District line traversed the city from east to west. With connecting lines it eventually served the northern outskirts in a rather indirect way. Even in the midst of this tangle of lines there was a need for better inner-city communications, particularly between the wealthy West End and the commercial centre.

The first proposal for such a line came in 1887. It was to run from St Enoch Square to Partick along a route to the north of that ultimately adopted. The track was to be interlaced in a 12ft 0in (3.7m) diameter tunnel, opening out to crossing loops at the stations which were to be 700yd apart. The trains, at 1400yd intervals, were to be permanently attached to the cable. This project went as far as a Parliamentary Bill, but this was defeated in the House of Commons. A more extensive scheme was put before Parliament in the following year for a circular route connecting the north and south banks of the river. This was defeated, largely on the grounds that tunnelling under the river at Yorkhill at the intended depth would inhibit further deepening of the river downstream of a proposed major dock development.

The way was opened for the subway promoters by the success of the Glasgow Harbour Tunnel Company in securing an Act in 1889 to build pedestrian and vehicular tunnels under the Clyde at Finnieston, up-river. A revised Bill was presented to Parliament in 1890, with the blessing of the burgh councils of Partick, Govan and Kinning Park, as well as of the University and the Trades' Council, and was passed. The main opposition came from the Caledonian Railway, which feared competition for its very expensive Glasgow Central Railway, by then under construction.

Unlike the London underground lines, which were constructed through the almost homogeneous London clay, the route of the subway lay through very mixed strata. Part of the line ran through sand and clay, and on these sections a shield was used, with compressed air to keep out water and mud. Where the ground above was soft, blowouts occasionally occurred, the most disastrous of which was in the bed of the Clyde south of St Enoch Station, which flooded the tunnels. Another serious accident occurred at St Enoch Square in December 1894, when a fire started in a pressurised section, owing to the accidental dropping of a candle in some wood. Fortunately, in this case the men trapped at the working face were rescued by breaking through from the adjacent tunnel but in a later, similar, accident at Govan two men were killed. Some parts of the route lay under public streets, and there the cut-and-cover method was employed, with piling sunk to form the sides of a trench wide enough to take the twin tunnels. The form of the tunnel roof was then excavated, the roof cast in concrete, the earth inside removed, and the sides and base of the tunnel cast. Of the 11,527yd (11,338m) of tunnel cut, about two-thirds were brick- or concrete-lined; the remainder through softer ground was lined with cast-iron sections, as used in the London tubes. The stations were all of the island-platform type, and were constructed mainly of wood. Not all of them were in tunnel. At Hillhead and Copland Road, for example, there were glazed roofs. Otherwise the stations were ill-lit and indeed rather depressing. The system, including its power station and car sheds, was completed during 1896, and opened on 14 December.

The public response was initially overwhelming. The opening day drew quite unexpected crowds, but was marred by two accidents, in one of which 18 people were injured. Services were immediately withdrawn, and not resumed until 21

January 1897. The system was advertised in a most attractive coloured poster boldly headed 'GLASGOW DISTRICT SUBWAY' and subtitled 'round the city in half an hour'. Views of a car interior and of a station exaggerated the amount of space on the narrow platform and in the diminutive cars, which were described as 'roomy and commodious'. The St Enoch station was the showpiece of the system. Dwarfed by its giant mainline neighbour, and even by the adjacent St Enoch Church, it was designed by the leading railway architect of the day, James Miller. *The Builder* in 1898 in a review of Glasgow's architecture described it as 'only a doll's house beside its big neighbour, but it is simply charming'.

The most remarkable feature of the little line was, however, the cable haulage system. Advertised as 'the only underground cable railway in the world—no smoke, no steam, perfect ventilation', it was powered by two steam engines, rated at 1500–2000hp, with 50-ton flywheels to even out the fluctuating load. Each engine could drive the system unaided. The cable from each tunnel was looped round two drive pulleys, and then through a tension run before re-entering the tunnel. The gripman on each car had to release the cable on the approach to the power station and pick it up immediately beyond. The cables weighed about 57 tons each, and lasted for about 90,000–180,000 miles—one to two years. Advantages of the cable system were its reliability and its ability to cope with occasional flooding.

The system prospered for its first five years, but in 1901 the electrification of the Glasgow Corporation Tramways was completed, to coincide with the international exhibition of that year. The new method of propulsion gave the tramways a decided competitive advantage. The electric cars were quick, clean, offered a frequent service, and were remarkably cheap. The subway, despite electric lighting of the carriages, was at best a gloomy alternative, though it was more attractive in most respects than the steam-worked underground railways. The system covered its costs, and paid a dividend of $\frac{1}{2}$ per cent or 1 per cent until 1919, but was hardly a great commercial success. It was not so much that the trams ate into existing traffic, more that a ceiling had been reached in 1899–1900. This was not markedly exceeded except during the exceptional years of World War I, until the change of ownership in the mid-1920s.

The Glasgow District Subway Railway Company, as it had become in 1914, slid into unprofitability in 1919 as a result of the rises in wages and materials costs during the war. Declining traffic in the post-war depression of 1920–1 made the company's position impossible, and in 1922, after prolonged negotiations, Glasgow Corporation bought the system for £385,000, a mere 5 per cent of the original capital. The subway was quickly assimilated into the Tramways Department. Plans for electrification were made, but it was not until 1932 that one car was experimentally converted to electric propulsion. After extensive trials the decision to electrify was made in 1933. Electrification was completed in December 1935, the total cost being £94,000, against the 1922 estimate of £1 million. Economy was achieved by retaining the old car bodies, by re-using the old rail as conductor rail and by continuing the lighting system used in cable days, involving pickup from a pair of 'tee-irons' mounted on the tunnel sides. The tramway power station at Pinkston provided the current for the revitalised subway, which was re-christened—on the London pattern—the Underground. Glaswegians, however, have clung to the name subway to this day.

The system as electrified in 1935 was substantially the subway of 40 years earlier. It had inherited many features of the days of cable operation, and when on 25 January 1974 it was announced that the underground was to be modernised it was still basically a Victorian system. Many visitors to the city probably never detected the system at all. Apart from St Enoch and West Street all the 15 stations were approached through inconspicuous entrances in tenement houses or offices. If one managed to find a station, one bought a ticket from a tiny booking office and descended a flight of stairs to a narrow island platform. The first impression was usually of the warm blast of air from the tunnels with its distinctive subway smell, and the next of the narrow gauge—4ft 0in (1.2m). When a train appeared, the small size of the stock surprised: one American visitor exclaimed 'Oh, what a cute toob'. Inside the train the red leather seats faced each other across the corridor. During rush-hours it was amazing how many people could cram into these tiny vehicles. The nominal capacity was 144 in a 2-car train, but this could be exceeded. Once under way the speed seemed at times alarming, but the impression given by the nearness of the tunnel walls was deceptive: speed was limited to 20mph. Another feature was the flickering of the lights, caused by pick-up of the lighting current from the parallel T-irons running along the tunnel sides.

The most remarkable features of the system were not obvious to the visitor. These were mainly hang-overs from cable days. One was the gradient profile, which was designed to provide a short steep slope up to each station to aid braking on entry and acceleration on departure. Much less convenient from an operating point of view was the arrangement for maintenance of the rolling stock. The work-shops at Govan were on the surface, with access to the tunnels by a pit just long enough to take a single car. All cars removed for regular maintenance or owing to breakdowns had to be lifted out of the pit by an overhead crane, and permanent way maintenance vehicles had to be lowered into the tunnels for their nocturnal work. Normally the work of lifting, though laborious, was quite quick. The crane was also used for turning the cars to allow them to operate on either circle. At one time, when the cars ran in a red-and-cream livery elaborately lined-out, the offside, never seen by the passengers, was painted unvarnished red, but latterly both sides were painted unlined red.

Elaborate procedures were devised for breakdowns in the tunnels. If a train lost power, but could be moved, the following train was allowed into the section and carefully moved up to the casualty. The two trains were then coupled by a wire-rope link, and the defective train pushed to the next station, where the passengers were deposited while the duo made its way to Govan. To speak to the nearest station each driver carried a portable telephone which could be clamped to the T-irons after the lighting current had been short-circuited. If the train was completely immobilised the current was cut-off from the live rail, a shorting bar was placed to link the live rail to the nearest running rail, and the passengers were led in groups to the nearest station.

Other peculiarities of the line included the method of collecting the takings from the booking offices. A special train was run immediately after the last public service, bringing the cash to Govan for banking. Not surprisingly, the line had its ghosts, mostly seen by the line walkers and pump men. There have been few serious accidents, though nine of the staff were killed between 1950 and 1975. The most dramatic incident affecting the subway was the bomb which struck Beith Street Bowling Green, near Merkland Street station, in September 1940. It shattered both cast-iron-lined tunnels, and the damage took four months to repair. In the final year (1975–6) of the old underground's operation the line was affected on a number of occasions by civil engineering work. The last and most serious of these deprived the Glasgow public of its expected orgy of nostalgia, in other words a formal last train ceremony.

So the old subway slipped away. Two cars are to find their way into Glasgow's transport museum, while the others have been scattered over the countryside—to Beamish, Midlothian, and even the Isle of Arran. The system was in the throes of reconstruction as this chapter was being written, and the first of the new generation of cars had been delivered. Most of the old peculiarities have gone, though they will live in the memories of countless Glaswegians. But the subway, reconstructed with the aid of a 75 per cent infrastructure grant from the Government, will rise, phœnix-like, from the ashes of the old system and will surely make for itself a new place in the affections of Scotland's greatest city.

# 8

# GOODS STATIONS

## The Goods Revolution 1830–1914

The first railway in Glasgow was probably the wooden tramway carrying coal in the 1750s from John Dixon's pits at Gartnavel and Knightswood to Yoker on the north bank for shipment by river to his glassworks at Dumbarton. The same family some 20 years later had a similar line connecting pits at Rutherglen with Springfield, part of the route of which was eventually utilised by the Polloc & Govan Railway. Authorised in 1830, this line opened for mineral traffic in 1840. So far as the Garnkirk & Glasgow Railway (Chapter 1) went, with Glebe Street as its terminus, there was little hope of satisfying the demand for coal increasingly being made by the booming steamer traffic on the river, or of supplying export markets. Although a line, partly in tunnel, from the G&G to the Broomielaw was projected in 1829, it was not built. The G&G was at an advantage in serving the growing heavy industries of Port Dundas and the northern industrial suburbs. It was no accident that immediately adjacent to the Townhead terminus was the St Rollox Chemical Works of Charles Tennant & Co— Charles Tennant was among the most active of the directors of the G&G. For a time from the 1830s St Rollox was the largest heavy chemical complex in the world, and by the 1840s took in 60,000 tons of coal per annum. Trucks were run in to the works on a high-level staging and the coal tipped through traps into carts below.

In 1848 the General Terminus & Glasgow Harbour Railway opened. This linked the Polloc & Govan with the Glasgow & Paisley Joint, the Glasgow Paisley Kilmarnock & Ayr, the Glasgow, Barrhead & Neilston Direct and the Clydesdale

Junction railways. Thus the south bank of the Clyde monopolised coal shipment. By 1888 along the 2000ft quay at General Terminus there were 14 turntables. The goods shed was 150ft 0in by 62ft 0in (45.7m by 18.9m) and an hydraulic engine house on the north west powered the nine dockside cranes:

**Table 11:    Cranes at General Terminus, 1888**

| Crane No | Manufacturers | Capacity (Tons) | Date installed | Cost (£) |
|---|---|---|---|---|
| 1 | Russell & Co | 30 | 1887 | 1,800 |
| 2 | Russell & Co | 30 | 1887 | 1,700 |
| 3 | Cowans Sheldon & Co | 30 | 1883 | 1,815 |
| 4 | Cowans Sheldon & Co | 20 | 1869 | 900 |
| 5 | John Yule & Co | 30 | 1876 | 1,525 |
| – | Chapman & Co | 1–4 (travelling) | – | 525 |

Mineral traffic was only one aspect of the goods revolution. Between 1840 and 1850 all the railway companies built goods sheds, sidings and warehouses at or near their passenger terminals, but as with the accommodation for passengers they proved too small. Both the North British (at Queen Street) and the Caledonian (at Buchanan Street) made the mistake of handling freight and passengers at the same depot. Although both companies embarked on rebuilding programmes in the 1860s, the heaviest capital expenditure was in the first decade of this century. By 1913 railway warehousing was not only big business, but had given the city a bold and modern functional architecture which is as worthy of study as the *art nouveau* of Charles Rennie Mackintosh. Unlike the passenger stations, there was no pressure to keep up appearances by following some quasi-historical architectural style. Increased floor loads, the use of more powerful hydraulic hoists, the advent of electric wagon traversers and similar equipment, necessitated a liberal use of brick, concrete and mild steel. Insurance companies liked the new materials for their fire-resisting qualities. However, the rise of the goods depot is more immediately appreciated if we look at the *Official*

*Handbook of Railway Stations* published by the Railway Clearing House:

Table 12:    Railway Stations and Private Sidings in Glasgow, 1877–1912

| Year | Passenger stations with goods depots | Goods stations | Private sidings | Crane power (Tons) goods stations only |
|---|---|---|---|---|
| 1877 | 9 | 17 | 4 | 150 |
| 1890 | 23 | 22 | 54 | 151 |
| 1912 | 29 | 52 | 183 | 638 |

Even this does not give the whole picture. *Reid's New Map of the River and Firth of Clyde* (1899) lists 263 important firms. Of these, the majority were on the 4½-mile stretch of the river bounded by Parkhead and Rutherglen on the east, and Partick and Govan on the west. This industrial concentration put an enormous strain on the railways. By 1910 the battle was won, but at a considerable environmental cost, over 820 acres (332ha) having been given over to marshalling yards, goods sheds and coal depots.

Once again, each of the 'big three' strove to establish a monopoly, and conflicts often bordered on the bizarre. Although the Edinburgh & Glasgow Railway Extensions Act (1864) had given the North British control of the Stobcross branch, the NB did all it could to make unworkable the running powers guaranteed to the Caledonian under this Act. Trouble began as early as 1 October 1874 when seven CR coal wagons destined for Dawsholm Gas Works Siding 'were only permitted to go forward as a special case' for running powers only applied to *stations* on the line. At this period, the only station on the branch other than those east of Sandyford Street was at Partick. Offers to 'accommodate' CR traffic here implied placing it entirely under NB control. Undaunted, the CR put in a 'movable office' and was brusquely told to take it away within three days. At last in 1876 the Caledonian got powers for a station of its own, but there was always an uneasy truce at Stobcross. To put in a siding at Partick in 1881, the Caledonian again went to Parliament, but there was a clause for the 'protection' of the

134

NB at Stobcross. When we see later on how the original Bill proposed an interesting change at Bellgrove, North British intransigence appears in a less bad light.

While coalmasters like the Dixons had backed the earliest industrial lines, so in the 1870s other strictly speaking non-railway interests took the initiative. The Whiteinch Railway was incorporated under the Companies Acts on 1 July 1872 to form

a branch railway or siding to communicate with the Stob-cross section of the North British Railway commencing at a point on the said Stobcross Section at or near the brickfield leased to Messrs Gilchrist & Goldie, and terminating on the Northside of the turnpike road leading from Glasgow to Dumbarton at or near the boundary between the estates of Scotstoun and Whiteinch, with a tramway or railway leading from the said railway through the estates of Scotstoun and Whiteinch and terminating at a point on the estate of Whiteinch near the shipbuilding yard belonging to Messrs Barclay Curle & Company.

The authorised capital was £18,000 and of the 16 original shareholders, 13 were shipbuilders. Although this company went into liquidation in 1881, it was managed by trustees until 1891 when it formally fell to the North British, though the tramway section remained privately-owned and managed until 1916. The Glasgow, Bothwell, Hamilton & Coatbridge Railway was promoted by a consortium of Lanarkshire steel-masters in 1874. Coatbridge had become the Sheffield of Scot-land, the blast furnaces of William Baird & Company of Gartsherrie alone then needed 400,000 tons (408,000 tonnes) of fuel a year to keep them at full capacity. The trouble was that the valuable splint coal and blockband ironstone seams in the Monklands and Wishaw areas. were virtually exhausted. The GBH&C was therefore designed to tap the relatively unexplored Bothwell fields. Great care was taken to point out that this was not an NB venture, yet Thomas Bouch, the NB consulting engineer, was strongly in favour of it, and the GBH&C was to have running powers over the Glasgow & Coatbridge line to College. Now both the NB and the G&SW had guaranteed the interest on £100,000 of College Station Stock, and all newcomers to the station were to pay tolls to the City of Glasgow Union Railway. When the CGU found no clear financial guarantees to them in the original GBH&C Bill, it took the latter to task. The point at issue was eventually settled amicably, but only after 1037 pages of Parliamentary evidence had been taken! The Caledonian, which dominated the Wishaw area, was trickier to deal with. Between 1873 and 1878 it had a 'new lines' agreement with the NB whereby 'neither company shall directly or indirectly promote or support any new line in the district of the other'. This did not prevent a Bill for railways at Newton Junction and St Rollox running parallel with the GBH&C. In 'self-defence' the North British then took over the GBH&C. A year later (1879) the Caledonian went to law, but scored on only a few minor points.

More ominous had been the Caledonian's attempt in 1881 (albeit unsuccessful) to get into the NB and G&SW siding adjacent to the city's cattle market at Bellgrove. Bellgrove siding was always difficult to work. With little room for expansion, the NB had to marshal its cattle trains at Sighthill or Camlachie. There could be delays of up to four hours, and traders with livestock from the north preferred to unload it at St Rollox, driving the beasts through the streets to market. The Caledonian was doing well enough already; as John Walker, the NB general manager, put it, the CR's real motive was 'to base a claim hereafter to run over and use the whole of the City Union & Coatbridge Line, and to occupy their spacious and important central stations'.

## The Early Goods Stations

Right from the start, Queen Street goods station was a magnet for east coast grain traffic. No drawings of the first buildings survive, but in June 1841 we find Messrs Turiff and Company agreeing to supply cast-iron columns at £7–0s–0d (£7.00) a ton. By 1844 the Town Council was demanding 'a screen to the granaries at the north side of Queen Street'. In 1847 the E&G got a shipping clerk to book 'all goods from Glasgow to Edinburgh' and resolved 'to alter the present system of working the grain traffic in Glasgow. The Company to work it by servants employed and paid by them instead of by Mr Gray'. Queen Street's success made it a congested and dangerous place (Chapter 4), and in the late 1850s the goods part was reconstructed. What happened is by no means clear, but the report of the company's engineer (December 1854) had much to say. The tunnel was to be opened and widened as far as Cathedral Street, houses on the west side of North Hanover Street were to be demolished—it would all cost 'about £40,000'. As an alternative, Adie mentioned a 'proposed line and station to Dobbies Loan' costing £126,000. It would occupy ten acres, but this (Chapter 4) suggested a surrender to the Caledonian. Ten acres (4.0ha) might be utilised at St Rollox but cartage would cost an extra £200 per year. The fourth proposal entailed taking a line from the tunnel to four acres (1.6ha) of E&G land at Parliamentary Road, but this would cost 'more than the improvement of the present station'. What improvements were made to Queen Street owed something to a relief of congestion brought about by the new goods station at Sighthill. Opened in July 1864, the yard at Sighthill was 'paved with stones cut down out of the old whinstone sleepers with which the Edinburgh & Glasgow line was originally laid . . . a handsome gateway leads down to a range of well designed well lighted and ventilated goods offices, beside which is the largest goods shed in the city, 360feet long, 150 broad [110.0 by 46.0m] and capable of containing 80 wagons'. If this was a revolution, its results were overestimated, for the merger of the E&G with the NB intensified the 'battle of the companies' and any foothold in George Square, the commercial heart of the city, was worthwhile.

Up to World War I the most important goods station in the city was at Buchanan Street (Fig 22). If we ignore General Terminus, we find that in 1890 it had the greatest available crane power (25 tons [25.5 tonnes]) of any station in Glasgow. In 1886 goods receipts totalled £141,413, but passengers only brought in £64,996. It was therefore no accident that the travelling public was neglected (Chapter 4) though at first, in 1849 the Caledonian would only have a goods shed 'if funds can be provided'. Although opened for goods on 1 January 1850, there was much pilfering 'attributable mainly to the reduced wages now paid' and discreet enquiries were made as to G&SW and E&G labour relations. The city fathers, too, had cause to complain, for no planning permission had been obtained for the goods offices, but since they were now built, they preferred not to act. Unfortunately, most plans lodged with the Glasgow Dean of Guild Court before 1885 have been destroyed, but tracings of those passed in 1864 for new buildings at the goods station are preserved in the Caledonian archives. The goods lines were extended in a southerly direction, and in the vicinity of Parliamentary Road Robert Ward (to the designs of George Graham) built a 9-bay goods shed

Fig 29   Sketch of granary, Buchanan Street Goods Station, in 1968. The scale of the building indicates the significance of grain traffic in the heyday of rail transport.

400ft 0in by 215ft 0in (122.0 by 65.5m) and a 5-storey granary with a double basement whose foundations rested on Arden lime concrete grouted into the solid rock (Fig 29). In both buildings, cast-iron columns took the vertical load, those in the goods shed also conveying rain water from the roof. The total cost including 'hydraulic apparatus' by Sir William Armstrong & Co was £43,493.

## College Goods Station (GSW)

Under section 31 of the City of Glasgow Union Railway Act (1871) the grounds of the old University of Glasgow were vested in the NB and the G&SW. To the north, the NB built a goods station which was subsequently to be known as High Street. To the south of this was the College Goods Station of the G&SW, which closed on 1 January 1968. In 1870 it had a goods shed 250ft 0in by 320ft 0in (76.2m by 97.5m) served by 12 tracks, eight platforms and three cart roads. On its eastern side there were 10 'landing inclines' and three wagon traversers. Fronting Graeme Street (now Bell Street) was a cattle wharf and coal yard. In 1880 College handled 168,261 tons (172,626 tonnes) of goods and 12,642 tons (12,895 tonnes) of minerals, the tonnages for 1900 were 308,364 (314,531 tonnes) and 18,532 (18,903 tonnes) respectively. In 1874 powers were obtained for extending the yard westwards giving a total available area of about 18 acres, but in doing so the company not only had to acquire a new site for College Church and pay for a new building erected 'according to a plan to be prepared by Campbell Douglas, architect in Glasgow' but ensure that the bodies in the churchyard were removed 'at the sight and to the satisfaction of the Medical Officer of Health of the City of Glasgow'. The old goods shed was swept away to allow for approach lines to a new one further west. It was 414ft 0in by 435ft 0in (126.8m by 132.6m) and had an undercroft and overhead store served by cranes and hoists powered by an hydraulic accumulator working up to 700lb/sq in (50atm). Between 2 January 1876 and 27 July 1883 not less than £108,242 had been spent on the station buildings alone.

## The Great Rebuilding 1890–1914

As long as Glasgow remained heavy engineer extraordinary to the British Empire, the goods system as a whole would continue to boom. Goods management became more complicated—in 1910 the Caledonian set up a special accounting office for the whole of the Glasgow area. Healthy public relations with the customer were essential, but sometimes the companies were totally unprepared for events. For example, a spate of tenement building at Shettleston in the 1890s had the North British station there 'jammed out' with builders' carts and trucks. Six hours per day were wasted shunting out individual empties. The Caledonian responded by building a new goods station at Tollcross. To redress the balance, the North British spent £3796 (exclusive of land) on a goods yard at Carntyne and loop to Parkhead which was ready for use by 17 September 1901.

The real headache was Sighthill. In 1898 it was storing on average 300 mineral wagons per day, while many more new and repaired wagons were kept bottled-up at Cowlairs. This was so ruining North British competitive traffic, that on one occasion the Great Northern felt inclined to suggest that the express goods from Sighthill to London be telegraphed from point to point like a fish train! At last in 1899–1900 North British plans (previously proposed in 1890) for a marshalling yard at Cadder, two miles (3.2km) north east of Bishopbriggs, were under way. Once let loose, the engineers had a field day. Buchanan Street would no longer have a monopoly, but the estimated costs were astronomical:

*Plates 23 and 24. (Above)* The concourse at Buchanan Street Station, *circa* 1960. *(Below)* A train from Aberdeen arriving at Buchanan Street in 1960. Tracks on the right led to the goods station. [*British Rail; John R. Hume*]

*Plates 25 and 26. (Above)* Glasgow Cross Station as built, with Sir J. J. Burnet's octagonal surface building. The railed enclosure in the foreground hides the shaft ventilating and lighting the station underground. The octagonal building was replaced *circa* 1923 by a smaller and simpler structure, when access to the High Street was improved. *(Below)* Underground at Glasgow Cross in 1962, with a Rutherglen-bound train about to depart. [*T. R. Annan & Son; John R. Hume*]

| | |
|---|---|
| College Goods Depot | £406,837 |
| College Coal Depot, Barrack Street | 32,938 |
| Sighthill Goods Sidings | 4,751 |
| Sighthill Goods Shed | 36,462 |
| Shettleston Sidings (up line) | 16,025 |
| Shettleston Sidings (down line) | 19,034 |
| Cadder Marshalling Sidings (up yard) | 65,085 |
| Cadder Marshalling Sidings (down yard) | 27,370 |
| | £608,522 |

Opened on 1 August 1907, College Depot (now known as High Street) was the largest and most up-to-date complex of its kind in Scotland (Figs 30, 31). Receipts for goods, minerals and coal leapt from £67,242 in 1912 to £356,448 in 1928. Contemporaries were fascinated by the 499ft 0in × 315ft 0in (162.0m × 96.6m) brick and steel warehouse whose third floor alone gave nearly 3½ acres (1.4ha) of storage. The ground floor was served by 10 pairs of rails and had five double-sided loading tables which could accommodate up to 160 wagons. To reduce fire risk, wagons in the building could be moved by 'no fewer than 30 electric capstans, each capable of exerting a pull of 1 ton (1.02 tonnes), or hauling about 100 tons (102 tonnes) on the level at a speed of 250ft/min (76.2m/min)'. These, and a host of electric cranes and wagon traversers were the brainchildren of A. W. Stewart, a Glasgow electrical engineer.

In August 1912 Cadder yard employed 36 marshalmen, guards and shunters, one signal lampman, six signalmen, an agent, and an assistant agent. Save for the last two who had houses in Bishopbriggs all commuted from Springburn, which by road is 3¼ miles (5.6km) from Cadder West. Owing to the 'crowded state of the line' the company would only put on a coach for men changing shifts at 6.00am and 6.00pm. Those coming off duty at 2.00pm, 4.00pm and midnight either

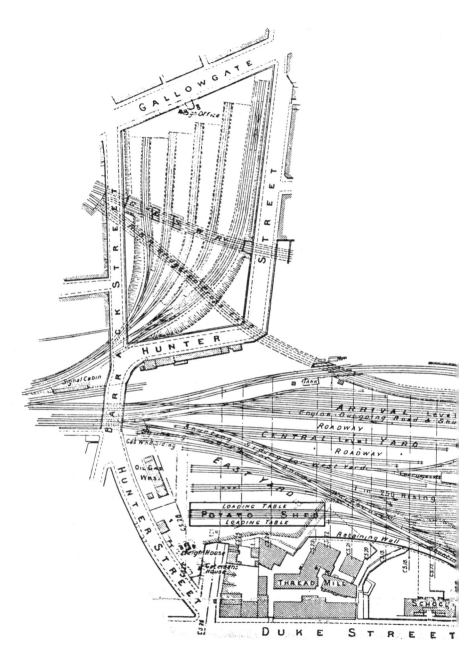

GALLOWGATE

*Gds. Office*

KELLY STREET

H U N T E R   STREET

*Signal Cabin*

B A R R A C K   S T R E E T

*Cal Whs. Sidings*

*Oil Gas Whs.*

HUNTER STREET

*Weigh House*

*Gatemans House*

*TANK*

ARRIVAL Level
*Engine Outgoing Road & Shu*
ROADWAY

CENTRAL Level YARD
ROADWAY

*Incoming Siding for West Yard*
E A S T   Y A R D

*Level*

1 in 250 Rising

POTATO SHED
LOADING TABLE
LOADING TABLE

*Receiving Well*

THREAD MILL

SCHOOL

D U K E   S T R E E T

walked home or took a lift on a goods train. This last practice was roundly condemned by Mr Black, superintendent of the line, for if even a 'simple incident like the bursting of a gauge glass in their faces was to happen, some of them who had no knowledge of such a thing might be tempted to leap off', and however slight the injury 'the state of affairs it fully revealed might not stand well on behalf of the Company'. Since certain employees had 'been heard to talk among themselves of a motor bus' the management wrote to 12 bus companies, but of these, only the Glasgow Motor Carriers Ltd sent in an offer to run one vehicle (but not on Sundays) at a charge of £1482 a year. The railway was more attracted to the alternative idea of paying for travelling time. It would only be £382 per annum but someone pointed out that still 'the men would surreptitiously find their way to and from the yard by means of the goods trains'. Company houses at Cadder were the answer and in October 1912 drawings were made of 'one and two room kitchen

Fig 30    Plan of High Street Goods Station as rebuilt, 1908. The main warehouse is on the right, with the Barrack Street coal depot on the top left.

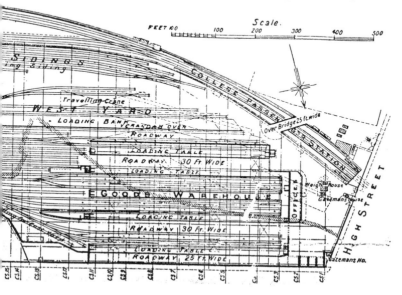

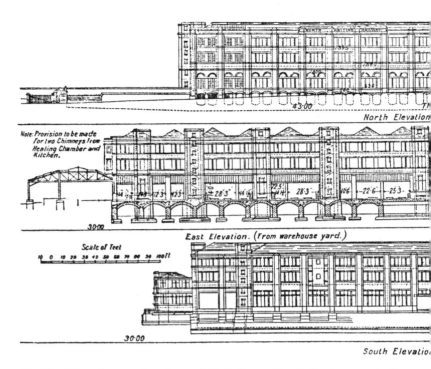

North Elevation

Note: Provision to be made for two Chimneys from Heating Chamber and Kitchen.

East Elevation. (From warehouse yard.)

Scale of feet

South Elevation

Fig 31    Elevations and sections of High Street Goods Station as rebuilt, 1908.

houses' for 20 tenants at a total estimated cost of £7785. Mr Black, condemning their wash hand-basins as needless luxuries, thought it would be a good idea to have a separate house for the stationmaster who would then 'be in a position to make surprise visits at different times during the day and night, and so exercise a better supervision of the staff generally'. Then Captain Stirling who owned the land would not have sewage effluent tipped down an old mine shaft, so the NB engineers looked for alternative building sites at Lenzie, Garngaber and Gallowhill. It was all becoming so expensive that in March 1914 the general manager was again thinking of buses, and the outbreak of war in August was just the thing to stop the bricks and mortar. The real wartime casualty was Sighthill Goods Depot whose receipts dropped from £91,847 in 1913 to £1299

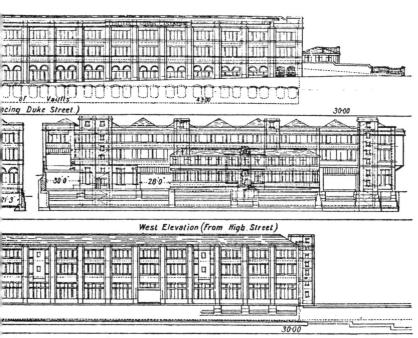

of Vaults

acing Duke Street.)

43·00

30·00

30·0

28·0

21·3

West Elevation (From High.Street.)

30·00

Facing Passenger Portion)

in 1918. Unknown to the general manager, high-ranking London officials had spied out the place on 30 September 1913, and from 5 August 1914 to early in 1919 it was an army supply depot. Ordinary traffic had to be diverted to High Street which quickly became congested. The real complaints came when a small shed at Sighthill was destroyed by fire. The army agreed to pay £73 in restitution but warned that this was not an 'official order for payment'. During World War II the burden again fell on the railways; in 1941 for example the Ministry of War Transport spent £50,650 on extending the Cadder yard. Apart from £60,000 authorised at Craigendoran, this was the heaviest expenditure on any LNER yard in Scotland between 1939 and 1942.

The railways and their warehouses also provided a vital link in the food chain of the city, for perishable food stuffs could be brought in bulk to the centre and rapidly distributed by networks of local wholesalers. In 1885 the G&SW viewed with dismay the Caledonian and North British monopoly of the grain traffic. The G&SW of course served the rich dairy region of south-west Scotland and noting that there was an intensive traffic in Glasgow of home-manufactured cheese amounting to probably 4000 tons (4080 tonnes), promptly re-equipped a warehouse near Gallowgate Station and 300yd (275m) from the city cheese market in South Albion Street. More remunerative were the gigantic bonded stores in Graeme Street (now Bell Street), which by 1895 had a floorage area of 82,000sq ft (7618m²). In the opinion of the *Victualling Trades Review*, G&SW goods traffic was 'regulated with the precision of clockwork'.

What was to be done with Buchanan Street Station? In 1900 the Caledonian secured powers for enlarging the bridge over Dobbies Loan and acquiring land at Parliamentary Road. The last caused considerable trouble, for proprietors demanded outrageous sums. From the outset it was agreed to pay the Glasgow Parish Council £90,000 for the old city poorhouse. Of this, about £4000 had to be paid back to the railway, for permission to remove two memorial tablets fixed in the wall of the main dining hall had provided the opportunity for stripping the place of all lead and other plumber work. Much of the poorhouse was never demolished. In 1909 the residue was converted into offices for the 90 clerks in the new goods accounting department and in 1910 remaining space was converted into tenements. As late as 1904, the directors could not make up their minds as to whether or not Buchanan Street should be turned over entirely to goods. The final decision (Chapter 5) may now seem short-sighted, but there were powerful trading interests to consider. Buchanan Street was the centre of the Glasgow potato market, in 1910 no fewer than six wholesalers renting space there. The new £78,000 potato shed at Dobbies Loan was ready for opening on 29 March 1909. Designed by Donald Matheson, its only notable feature was the structural steelwork, the roof having lattice girders of the 'N' type like those in the new Central Station. Three-foot (0.9m) high cast-iron lettering proclaimed that this was 'Buchanan Street Goods Station', but apart from the potato merchants nobody cared for the warehouse on the second storey, which in 1913 did not even have a 30cwt (1.52 tonne) electric crane for Messrs Pilkington's glass crates, while the proximity of the old E&G tunnel to Queen Street inevitably entailed limited basement accommodation. The potato sidings cost £8500, but Matheson's plan to spend a similar figure on lowering the level of the ground between the new and old goods yards was frowned on. Little wonder then that the technical press dwelt on the North British complex in the High Street. The Caledonian's Central Station was still the queen of passenger terminals, but in building it something had to be sacrificed elsewhere.

### The Post-war Pattern

While countless passenger stations succumbed early to the tram and the motor car, most continued to handle freight. Just as the goods network began with minerals so it ended, for by the 1950s the domestic coal fire was no longer a necessity. This, plus a decline in the traditional heavy industries, signalled the death warrant for no fewer than 75 depots in the years 1954–69. Included was Queen Street Goods which at last closed on 6 January 1964. Furthermore, Glasgow is now the great motorway city, and significantly the only major new investments in freight handling have been the opening of a freightliner terminal on the site of the former Caledonian mineral yard at Gushetfaulds in December 1967, and the re-equipping of General Terminus to handle shipments of iron-ore for the Lanarkshire blast furnaces in 1957, itself soon to be superseded.

149

# 9

# ENGINEERS
# AND ARCHITECTS

The design of the simple, early terminals in Glasgow, as elsewhere, was often classical, regular or irregular, at least to the
casual observer. The restricted sites of terminals near the
centre imposed their own constraints on design, especially
where an expensive, vaulted undercroft was an essential feature, as at St Enoch and Central stations. The construction of
new termini, and the reconstruction of old, involved sophisti-
cated study of traffic flows, of economical means of sheltering
and lighting large areas, and of the provision of ancillary facilities, such as hotels, parcels offices and refreshment rooms.
While there was a growing body of experience among architects in the design of large railway stations, gained mainly from
London and foreign cities, the influence of this expertise on the
Glasgow stations appears to have been remarkably slight.
Only St Enoch was directly influenced by London practice,
and even it was no slavish copy. The sturdy independence of
the Scottish railway companies was in this field reinforced by
the existence of vigorous local architectural and structural engineering professions. Glasgow architects were few in number
and not particularly important in the eighteenth century, but
during the nineteenth century, when the city was expanding
most rapidly, the architectural opportunities available created
a climate in which local talent flourished. Men like Alexander
'Greek' Thomson, Sir J. J. Burnet, and Charles Rennie Mackintosh became renowned far outside the city for domestic and
ecclesiastical architecture, but others, such as James Miller,
were responsible for functional, economical and graceful
buildings for railway and other purposes. Even the engineers'

departments of the railway companies could produce competent designs, Donald Matheson of the Caley being particularly important.

The competition among architects became increasingly fierce in the later nineteenth century—there were 36 architects in Glasgow in 1857 and 166 firms in 1897—and as buildings of ever-greater magnificence appeared in the commercial centre, while in the residential suburbs there was an incentive to the railway companies to engage in architectural display as a weapon in the battle for traffic. The North British did not really enter the ring, but there was modest competition between the G&SW and the Caley; the latter, in paralleling the NB for north-bank suburban traffic, commissioned the finest series of suburban stations north of the border for the Glasgow Central and Lanarkshire & Dumbartonshire lines (see Chapter 6). The competitive spirit was less obviously expressed in the main-line terminals, though it was undeniably there. It is interesting to note that the St Enoch and Central Hotels were designed by 'foreign' architects, though the architectural work for the Central extension of 1901–5 was by local man James Miller.

In contrast, the engineers of Glasgow's stations were frequently drawn from outside the region. Sir John Fowler as chief consultant for St Enoch is a prime example; his contractors, Thomas Brassey & Co, and their subcontractors for the ironwork, Handyside of Derby, made the enterprise peculiarly English. The involvement of Blyth & Cunningham, Edinburgh civil engineers, in the first Central station, and of Sir John Barry in the second is also notable, especially as by 1897 Glasgow had at least 120 professional civil engineers. Only Donald Matheson stands out as a man practising locally, though William Melville's work on the extension of St Enoch was competent enough and well-regarded at the time, while James Carswell's Queen Street was notably economical.

The following brief biographical sketches of some of the more important architects and engineers associated with the building of Glasgow's stations are included to help to place their Glasgow work in a wider context, and to show how men of different technical backgrounds combined to solve the problems involved in moving ever larger numbers of passengers and greater volumes of goods. The figures quoted for their estates refer only to *movable* property held in Britain.

## Architects

*Sir Robert Rowand Anderson (1834–1921)*   Anderson's practice was always firmly entrenched in Edinburgh. If some of his buildings appear odd and antiquarian, this is not true of his Central Station (1875–83), his only railway project. Here he made the acquaintance of Blyth & Cunningham (*qv*) who were later to do the engineering calculations for the roof of the baroque McEwan Hall in Edinburgh. Anderson left over £65,000.

*Sir John James Burnet (1857–1938)*   Born in Glasgow. At the age of 18 he went to Paris where he rapidly distinguished himself at the Ecole des Beaux Arts. His father, John Burnet (1814–1901), had given Glasgow at least 14 major public buildings. However, John Burnet junior was to give the firm a national reputation. Although he is chiefly remembered for his additions to the British Museum (1904) his devotion to functional truth is well expressed in the following: ventilating openings for the Glasgow Central Railway, Glasgow Cross and Kirklee Stations, 1895, Kelvinside Station 1896–7, Central Low Level Station 1897–1900, Anderston Cross Station 1899, buildings at Saltmarket and London Road 1902. In 1909 and 1910 he designed the new façade for shops fronting Argyle Street. Success persuaded him to move to London in 1905. Following World War I he was chief Architect to the War Graves Commission. He left £13,725.

*James Collie (?–c1870?)*   Is remembered for his superb neo-

Grecian façade at Bridge Street Station (1841). In 1858 he came second in the Buchanan Street Station competition. This plan was not carried out. In 1869 he designed Montrose Infirmary. Collie was Glasgow's first real station architect, but by 1864 he had left the city and retired in obscurity to Belmore House, an Italianate villa at Bridge of Allan.

*Miles Septimus Gibson (?–1906)*     The Glasgow architect who ably assisted Thomas John Willson of Hampstead (1823–1903) in designing the St Enoch Station Hotel. Both were church architects—Gibson designed various episcopal churches in Lanarkshire—but unlike Scott who made his mark at St Pancras, they had little experience in commercial projects. Why the G&SW employed them still remains a mystery. Gibson left £2305–7–8d (£2305.38).

*James Miller (1860–1947)*     If the champion of a new approach to station design was Donald Matheson, it was Miller the architect who gave the vital finishing touch. For George Graham (*qv*) he probably designed the huge Queen Anne façade to Bridge Street Station in 1888. He had started his own practice in 1893 and that same year on 25 July he agreed to design Botanic Gardens Station at a commission of $2\frac{1}{4}$ per cent. Although an art nouveau 'oriental' fantasy, it met the requirements of both the Caledonian and its environmental opponents. As one contemporary said: 'he had no special preference to any particular class of work, much of his success might be attributed to his ability to look at the problem from his clients' point of view'. Commissions soon flowed in. As well as St Enoch Subway Station, 1896, he designed stations on the West Highland Railway, Princes Pier, and Gourock Stations. The railway hotels at Turnberry and Gleneagles are his masterpieces, and the surviving drawings show a tremendous grasp of planning and technical detail. He also designed the Glasgow International Exhibition Buildings (1901), a museum at Bombay (1908), and the new building for the Institution of

Civil Engineers in London. Miller was one of those few architects who did not get into the bad books of the Caledonian. Like him, Matheson was also born in Perthshire, and had had some early architectural training. Miller left over £40,000.

*Sir William Tite (1798–1873)* Architect to the London & Southampton Railway and the London & Birmingham Railway, his grand Glasgow schemes for the Caledonian (p 93) came to nothing. Tudor gothic elevations of the present Perth General Station (by Tite and his assistant Ebenezer Trotman) were approved by Locke on 27 April 1847. Trotman had designed a church in Tewkesbury in 1837, by 1848 he had hit upon a standardised form of tank house to be used at stations on the Scottish Central.

## Engineers

*James Fairie Blair (1831–76)* Trained under John Miller and worked under John Fowler on railway projects in the west and north-west of Ireland, later becoming consulting engineer to the Minho District Railway of Portugal. By 1863 he had returned to Edinburgh and set up in private practice. Almost immediately he got the job of engineering the City of Glasgow Union Railway, but the physical and mental strain proved too much, and he died while convalescing at Schuls Unter Engadin in Switzerland. He left £18,849.

*Benjamin Hall Blyth (1819–66)* In the early 1850s Blyth, who had trained under Grainger & Miller (*qv*), opened an office at 135 George Street, Edinburgh. With his brother Edward he quickly established a reputation as a consulting engineer. Work flowed in from the G&SW, the Scottish Central, the Dundee & Perth, the Great North of Scotland, and the Portpatrick companies. Number 135 became Edinburgh's 'Westminster'. Above all, the Caledonian was quick to appreciate the firm's reputation for efficiency and thoroughness. Blyth died from overwork, leaving just over £56,000. In 1914 Benjamin Hall (his eldest son) had the distinction of being the first engineer practising in Scotland to be elected President of the Institution of Civil Engineers. As far as railways are concerned, the years 1870–1900 were the firm's busiest. Work carried out included the first Glasgow Central Station and approach lines, the Balerno and Uddingston branches of the Caledonian, the Callander and Oban line and large-scale remodelling Carlisle Citadel, Perth General, and Waverley stations.

*James Carswell (c1833–97)*   In 1869 Carswell succeeded Deas as resident engineer of the western section of the North British Railway, becoming engineer-in-chief from 1879. Queen Street Station roof remains his masterpiece. He engineered the Forth Bridge approach lines, and was responsible for many buildings on the West Highland Railway, including workmen's houses at Fort William (1895). He left £6567.

*William Crouch (1840–1921)*   Glasgow consulting engineer in partnership with C. P. Hogg (*d* 1927) who acquired J. F. Blair's practice in 1876. Crouch trained under John Fowler in London and was for a time employed by the Metropolitan Railway. Crouch and Hogg were responsible for such projects as the Alloa Railway, and the Lochearnhead, St Fillans & Comrie Railway. Hogg left £19,564, Crouch's estate came to £80,174.

*James Deas (1827–99)*   From 1869 he was chief engineer to the Clyde Trust. Although the Trustees and the railways frequently came to blows, no one could deny that in the long run, Deas' activities benefited everyone. Quayage increased from 3.18 to 18¼ miles (5.2–29.7km) and the water area from 76 to 209 acres (30.7–84.5ha). His greatest single project was probably the Princes Dock (1887–96) which from 1899 was being served by the CR, G&SW and the NBR. Deas came from a railway background. A pupil of John Miller, for a short time, he was engineer-in-chief to the E&G, a post his father had also held and later to the Glasgow District of the NB. He left £8571.

155

*Robert Dundas (1838–97)*    Trained under Charles Ower, harbour engineer, Dundee, and B. H. Blyth. In 1866 he became principal assistant to George Graham (*qv*). While resident engineer to the Glasgow & Paisley and Glasgow & Kilmarnock Joint Lines (1871–80) he enlarged the then inadequate goods stations.

*James R. Forman (1822–1900)*    A native of Nova Scotia (but of Scottish descent), in the 1840s he worked on the construction of the Wilsontown Morningside & Coltness Railway. In 1860, he entered into partnership with Messrs Robson and McCall, to form the firm of Formans & McCall, which rapidly established itself as one of the most active civil engineering consultancies in the West of Scotland. He was joined in 1874 by his son Charles (1852–1901) who had just completed his training under James Deas. Among the lines for which the firm was consultant were the Foxdale Railway in the Isle of Man, the Glasgow Central Railway and the West Highland. According to his obituary in *Engineering* (15 February 1901) Charles 'introduced in most of his lines the island platform and broke through conventions with his buildings, giving a wayside station an aesthetic picturesqueness foreign to the prevailing dinginess of most of our country railway buildings'. He left £81,083.

*George Graham (1822–99)*    Born at Hallhills, Dumfriesshire, he began his career as an apprentice with Robert Napier of Glasgow, working on the engines of the first Cunarders. Resigning for reasons of health, he never returned to mechanical engineering. In 1845 he found employment as an 'amateur assistant' to Joseph Locke on the Caledonian Railway, and on 10 September 1847 Graham was given the privilege of starting the locomotive which hauled the first public passenger train from Beattock to Carlisle. From 1 August 1853 to his death (he died on the day of his retirement) he was the Caledonian's engineer-in-chief, but apart from a privately-printed account of the early history of the Company, Graham published virtually nothing, and only became a member of the Institution of Civil Engineers in 1889. A most shy person, he was not good at giving evidence before committees, yet his name appears in connection with most matters involving the safety and maintenance of the Company's permanent way. He was responsible for seven bridges across the River Clyde; that at Dalmarnock in 1861 was one of the first in Scotland to have wrought iron bowstring girders resting on cast-iron piers. Very remarkable working drawings (dated 1862) survive of his scheme for strengthening the viaduct (at the time one of the highest in Britain) carrying the Lesmahagow branch over the Nethan Water. In 1884 he planned the extension from Greenock to Gourock, which gave the Caledonian a strong lead in the competition for Clyde Coast pleasure traffic. At his death he left estate worth over £29,000.

*Donald Alexander Matheson, (1860–1935)*   Born at Perth, he was educated at the Academy there, subsequently passing on to Heriot Watt College, Edinburgh (now Heriot Watt University). Joining the London & North Western Railway, he held the post of assistant engineer in the Lancashire and Yorkshire district between 1884 and 1886, at the same time attending classes at Owens College Manchester. In 1886 he joined R. McAlpine, the contractor for the Lanarkshire & Ayrshire Railway and in 1890 was appointed at the resident engineer responsible for the Central Low Level Lines of the Caledonian Railway then under construction. Following the death of George Graham (*qv*) in 1899, he became engineer-in-chief. Three years later he went on a fact-finding mission to the USA. Subsequently he represented the Caledonian at the International Railway Congress at Berne. In 1910 he became the company's general manager.

As early as 1912 Matheson had been an ex-officio member of the Communications Board set up by the War Office and the Board of Trade. In 1916 he visited the Somme to draw up plans for sending British railway materials and expertise to France.

He was chiefly responsible for carrying through the construction of Gleneagles Hotel, one of the Caledonian's most successful projects. Planned by James Miller in 1913, completion of the hotel was delayed by the outbreak of war. Following the regroupings of 1923 he was deputy general manager of LMS (Scottish Region) until his retirement in 1926. His contribution to station design has been underestimated; although the reconstructed Central Station is his masterpiece, modified designs based on it appeared elsewhere, as for example in his proposals of October 1909 (which were unanimously accepted) for rebuilding the roof of Perth General Station. He frequently referred to the station 'concourse', an American term quite new to his fellow Scottish engineers.

In 1887 he became an associate member of the Institution of Civil Engineers, in 1895 he was elected a member. He had the distinction of holding both the James Watt and George Stephenson medals of this body. Most of the official photographs of Matheson show him looking worried and depressed (Plate 30), but this was certainly not true when he travelled on the Royal Train in Scotland, a duty he performed without a break for nearly 30 years. At his death he left estate worth just over £43,000.

*William Melville (1850–1920)*    Born in Dunoon, and apprenticed to a joiner, then spending a period in a Glasgow engineer's office before joining the North British Railway. Here he was appointed assistant to James Carswell (*qv*) and worked on the extension of Queen Street Station, where he had a hand in the designing of the roof. He was also responsible for the work of enlarging Cowlairs Locomotive Works. In 1882 Melville became assistant to George Graham (*qv*) working on the widening of the Argyle Street bridge and the approach lines to Bridge Street Station, as well as supervising the construction of the Gourock extension. He was appointed chief engineer to the

*Plates 27 and 28. (Above)* Office block and station house, Hyndland Station, after closure in 1970. *(Below)* Up platform building at Crookston Station, built in 1885, when the Glasgow Paisley & Johnstone Canal was converted to a railway by the G&SW. The delightful glazed screen is unusual. [*Both, John R. Hume*]

*Plates 29 and 30. (Above)* Westerton Station in 1960, with an electric train on crew training before the start of regular services. The basic nature of the station buildings is evident. *(Below)* Donald A. Matheson, Engineer-in-Chief of the Caledonian Railway; the greatest of the Glasgow station designers. [*John R. Hume; British Rail*]

Glasgow & South Western Railway in 1891, and designed the extension to St Enoch Station. He was responsible for the reconstruction of Greenock Prince's Pier Station, and for the new locomotive sheds and railwaymen's houses built at Corkerhill between 1899 and 1901. He retired in 1916, and left an estate of £13,984.

*John Miller (1805–83)*    Very much the leading Scottish railway engineer in the 1840s, but so far he has had no biographer. Born at Ayr, he settled in Edinburgh, and after a spell at the university there, went into partnership with Thomas Grainger (1794–1852). The Monkland & Kirkintilloch, the Dundee & Arbroath, the Arbroath & Forfar, the Edinburgh & Hawick, the Stirlingshire Midland Junction, the Edinburgh & Glasgow, the Glasgow, Paisley, Kilmarnock & Ayr all bear witness to his amazing competence. For the last company, he designed at Ballochmyle near Mauchline a 181ft 0in (55.2m) span masonry arch, still the largest of its kind in Britain. In this work he was assisted by his nephew George M. Cunningham, later associated with Benjamin Hall Blyth (*qv*). In 1846 Miller was employed by the GPK&A and the E&G to engineer a West of Scotland Junction Railway in an endeavour to improve terminal facilities in Glasgow. A competent architect, his earliest known architectural drawing is of a coke shed at Kilwinning Station. Although better-class work could be found at Bridge Street Station in Glasgow and on the Edinburgh, Leith & Granton Railway, in 1847 he could still turn his hand to designing cast-iron mileposts and gradient marks for the Scottish Central. Retiring from practice in 1849 (he left £37,475 on his death) he purchased an estate at Innerleithen in Peebleshire. From 1868–74 he represented Edinburgh in Parliament.

*Neil Robson (1808–69)*    Born in Ayrshire, he was apprenticed to David Smith, civil engineer and land surveyor in Glasgow. He set up in business on his own in 1833, and surveyed several branches from the Monkland mineral lines. The Garn-kirk Railway employed him to design two connecting rail-ways, including the abortive Buchanan Street scheme. During the Railway Mania he proposed several railways, including the Glasgow, Dumbarton & Helensburgh, Glasgow, Barrhead & Neilston Direct and General Terminus and Glasgow Harbour lines. He was also engineer of the Lesmahagow branch of the Caledonian Railway. Marriage into the Merry family led to an extensive connexion with the iron industry, culminating in 1860 with his retirement from the engineering profession to take part in the management of Merry & Cunninghame, one of the largest coal and iron firms in Scotland.

## Contractors

*Sir William Arrol (1839–1913)*      Born at Houston, Renfrew-shire and employed in textile mills before apprenticeship to a Paisley blacksmith. Worked as a boilermaker until 1869 when he set up his own business in Bridgeton, Glasgow, where he founded the Dalmarnock Ironworks in 1872. His first major bridge contract was for a viaduct at Hamilton for the Glasgow, Bothwell Hamilton & Coatbridge Railway which was quickly followed by the Clyde viaduct leading to Central Station (1875–8). His firm was also responsible for the new viaduct added in 1901–5. Its most famous works are certainly the Forth and Tay railway bridges and Tower Bridge, London. Arrol was knighted for his work on the Forth Bridge, and was Liberal Unionist MP for South Ayrshire from 1895 to 1906. He left £316,589.

*Walter MacFarlane (1817–85)*      Established in 1850, throughout most of the century, Walter MacFarlane & Co specialised in a wide range of cast-iron building components. Highly ornate urinals and drinking fountains became a speciality, but modernisation has swept most of these MacFar-lane gems out of Glasgow's stations. The entrance to

MacFarlane's new warehouse under Cannon Street Station in London (1868) was typically festooned with ornament from his Glasgow foundry. He left £104,818.

*Walter MacLellan (1815–89)*     Senior partner of P. & W. MacLellan Ltd, Clutha Works, Glasgow. In business as hardware merchants at least as early as 1811, by 1860 the firm was specialising in iron and steel bridgework, probably casting some of the columns for the Gare du Nord in Paris (1863). In 1868 it supplied the components for Col. G. Collyer's and R. M. Ordish's suspension bridge at Singapore. MacLellan was the contractor for the present arched roof at Queen Street Station, and though designed by James Carswell and William Melville (*qv*) it is possible that Ordish, who worked on the iron arch at St Pancras Station in London, may have assisted with the calculations. He left £39,377.

*Watt & Wilson*     Had a yard and office at Petershill, Glasgow. On 22 April 1878 the firm obtained the main contract for building the first Central Station. Later employed at Hartwood by the Lanarkshire Lunacy Board, and in 1894 worked for the North British Railway at Abbeyhill in Edinburgh. In 1892 the firm won the Glasgow District Subway contract No 7. Also built the Thirlmere aqueduct for Manchester Corporation Waterworks. Following the retirement of Mr Wilson, this firm was dissolved on 30 September 1895.

*James Young & Sons*     In regular business from 1866, this Edinburgh firm had its navvies busy remodelling Queen Street Station in 1879. Contractors for Helensburgh Pier, Waverley Station and the mid-Lanarkshire and Ayrshire lines, by the late 1890s it was carrying out part of the Talla contract of the Edinburgh & District Water Trustees. Became a limited company on 2 March 1899, but liquidation and bankruptcy soon followed.

# ACKNOWLEDGEMENTS

The authors would like to thank the following for their assistance and advice in the preparation of this book: Messrs Blyth & Blyth, and in particular Miss M. J. Fergusson; British Rail; The Scottish Record Office, and in particular the Keeper of the Records of Scotland, Dr John Imrie; the Strathclyde Regional Archivist, Mr Richard Dell and his staff; and Messrs I. H. Adams, G. R. Barbour, J. F. McEwan, M. S. Moss, J. Shaw Dunn, and D. M. Walker. Miss Catherine Summerhill and Miss Carolyn MacLean typed the manuscript, often from illegible drafts.

The authors are also most grateful to the following for permission to reproduce illustrations: Messrs T. & R. Annan; Messrs Blyth & Blyth; British Rail (Scottish Region); Messrs Clark Chapman—John Thompson Ltd; The Pennycook Patent Glazing Co Ltd; Scottish Railway Preservation Society; and the Strathclyde Regional Archivist. Other sources of the Figures are acknowledged to *Engineering, The Engineer*, Scottish Record Office, Institution of Civil Engineers, Institution of Engineers and Shipbuilders in Scotland.

# BIBLIOGRAPHY

## Manuscripts

The manuscripts consulted are too numerous to list in detail here, but include minute books of the Caledonian; Edinburgh & Glasgow; Glasgow, Bothwell, Hamilton & Coatbridge; Glasgow & Paisley Joint; Glasgow & South Western; and North British railways. Correspondence files, newspaper cuttings books, plans and miscellanea in the British Rail Archives, Scottish Record Office, Edinburgh have also been used, in addition to plans in the Scottish Record Office's own series.

## Books and Articles

The books in this list have been included either because they are useful or important sources, or because they place Glasgow developments in context. The articles are either valuable contemporary accounts or significant recent histories.

### *Books*

Acworth, W. M., *The Railways of Scotland*, London, 1890
Casely, Gordon, and Hamilton, Bill, *I Belong to Glasgow: The Human History of the Glasgow Underground,* Glasgow, 1975
Ellis, C. Hamilton, *The North British Railway*, London, 1955
Gardner, J. W. F., *London Midland & Scottish Railway: Origins and Subsequent Development of the Railways in Scotland*, 1934
Gomme, Andor, and Walker, David, *The Architecture of Glasgow*, London, 1968

Highet, Campbell, *The Glasgow & South Western Railway*, Lingfield, Surrey, 1965

Hume, John R. *The Industrial Archaeology of Glasgow*, London & Glasgow, 1974

Kellett, John, *Railways and the Victorian City*, London, 1969

Lewis, M. J. T., *Early Wooden Railways*, London, 1970

Meeks, Carroll L. V. *The Railway Station*, London, 1957

Nock, O. S., *The Caledonian Railway*, London, 1961

Smith, David L., *Tales of the Glasgow & South Western Railway*, London, n.d.

Stephenson Locomotive Society, *The Caledonian Railway Centenary 1847–1947*, London, 1947

Stephenson Locomotive Society, *The Glasgow & South Western Railway 1850–1923*, London, 1950

Thomas, D. L., and Sinclair, D. E., *The Glasgow Subway*, Scottish Tramway Museum Society, Glasgow, 1964

Thomas, John, *The North British Railway*, Vols. 1 & 2, Newton Abbot, 1969 and 1975

Thomas, John, *Regional History of the Railways of Great Britain: Scotland, The Lowlands and the Borders*, Newton Abbot, 1971

Thomas, John, *The Springburn Story*, Newton Abbot, 1964

Whishaw, Francis, *Railways of Great Britain and Ireland*, London, 1840

*Articles*

General

Langmuir, G. E., 'Closed Stations in Glasgow', *The Railway Magazine*, January 1938

Kellett, J. R., 'Glasgow's Railways, 1830–80: a Study in Natural Growth', *The Economic History Review*, 2nd Series, 17 (1964), 360–2

Introduction

Gourvish, T. R., 'The Railways and Steamboat Competition in Early Victorian Britain', *Transport History*, 4, 1964, 1

Chapter 2

Blyth, Benjamin Hall, 'The Caledonian Railway Viaduct over the River Clyde at Glasgow', *Mins of Procs Inst CE*, LXI, 1879–80, p.000

Gairns, J. F., 'Central Station and Traffic Arrangements', *Railway Magazine*, October 1923, 285

Hutchinson, E. Boyd, 'The Electro-pneumatic signalling installation at Central Station,' *The Railway Magazine*, November 1908, 380

Lawrence, J. T., 'Glasgow Central', *The Railway Magazine*, January, 1907, 1

Matheson, D. A., 'Glasgow Central Station Extension', *Mins of Procs Inst CE* CLXXV, 1909, 30–184

Robin, G. H., 'The History of Glasgow Central', *Railway World*, February 1963, 53, March 1963, 102

Travis, Charles, 'Glasgow Central', *The Railway Magazine*, September 1923, 169

Chapter 3

Gairns, J. F., 'St Enoch Station', *Railway Magazine*, January 1925, 1

Hogg, Charles P., 'On St Enoch Railway Station', *Tr I of E&S in S*, 25 (1881–2), 193–202 and 26 (1882–3), 33–4

Lawrence, J. L., 'The Extension of St Enoch Station', *The Railway Magazine*, September 1904, 248

Melville, W., 'City Union Railway Widening and Extension of St Enoch Station', *Tr I of E&S in S*, 44 (1900–1), 222–62

Robin, G. H., 'The City of Glasgow Union Railway', *The Railway Magazine*, 1960, 20–26

Robin, G. H., 'St Enoch Station, Glasgow', *Railway World*, January 1962, 19–25

Tarbet, Smellie, 'St Enoch Station', *The Railway Magazine*, February 1902, 164

Whitechurch, Victor, L. 'How the traffic is worked at St Enoch Station', *The Railway Magazine*, January 1899, 22

**Chapter 4**

Calder, J., 'Queen Street Station', *The Railway Magazine*, February 1901

Gairns, J. F., 'Queen Street Station', *The Railway Magazine*, January 1930, 1

**Chapter 5**

Gairns, J. F., 'Buchanan Street Station', *The Railway Magazine*, January 1928, 1

McEwan, J. F., 'An Unusual Engineering feature in Glasgow', *The Railway Magazine*, January, 1953, 46

**Chapter 6**

Robin, G. H. 'The Lanarkshire & Ayrshire Railway', *The Railway Magazine*, February, 1961, 89–96

Robin, G. H., 'The Lanarkshire & Dunbartonshire Railway', *The Railway Magazine*, January 1959, 19–20

Robin, G. H., 'The South Side Suburban Railways of Glasgow', *The Railway Magazine*, January 1954, 9–15, 17 and February 1954

Simpson, Robert, 'On the Construction of the Glasgow City & District Railway', *Tr I of E&S in S*, 31, 1887–8, 97–121

**Chapter 8**

Anon., 'High Street Goods Station', *The Railway Magazine*, January 1921

Waddell, M., 'The Caledonian Railway's Diamond Jubilee: The Goods Department', *The Railway Magazine*, September 1907, 221

# INDEX

171